Fannie de Miller

Snap Notes of an Eastern Trip

Fannie de Miller

Snap Notes of an Eastern Trip

ISBN/EAN: 9783337124755

Printed in Europe, USA, Canada, Australia, Japan

Cover: Foto ©Andreas Hilbeck / pixelio.de

More available books at **www.hansebooks.com**

SNAP NOTES

OF

AN EASTERN TRIP

FROM DIARY OF

FANNIE DE C. MILLER

"When found, make a note of"
—*Captain Cuttle*

SAN FRANCISCO
THE S. CARSON COMPANY
PUBLISHERS AND BOOKSELLERS,
1892

To
My Sisters, Nellie, Tessie and Josie, who afforded me
the trip, and Mrs. B. D. Murphy, who
added to its
enjoyment, I dedicate these straggling
notes as a slight souvenir of my appreciation of the
pleasure experienced.

PREFACE.

IN presenting these hastily snatched notes for perusal my friends will generously bear in mind the fact that no attempt at literary effort is intended. Having had the benefit of the trip and enjoyed it, I reproduce some of the leaves of my diary for private circulation, and may be pardoned for so doing since it is commemorative of my first visit outside the bounds of the California peninsula. That many pages of this little book may contain faults I readily acknowledge and must regret, in view of my motto, *Scriptum manet*.   F. DE C. M.

CONTENTS.

		PAGE.
I.	OVER THE RANGE	9
II.	FROM OGDEN EAST OVER THE DENVER AND RIO GRANDE	17
III.	FROM DENVER TO DETROIT	32
IV.	A VISIT TO NIAGARA	45
V.	THE CITY OF BOSTON	58
VI.	GLIMPSES OF NEW YORK	75
VII.	A TRIP UP THE HUDSON	88
VIII.	THE CITY OF BROTHERLY LOVE	96
IX.	A VISIT WITH CARDINAL GIBBONS	102
X.	ROSELAND AND ENNISCORTHY, TYPICAL SOUTHERN HOMES	108
XI.	SCENES IN GETTYSBURG	115
XII.	THE CITY OF EMMITTSBURG, THE OLD HOMESTEAD AT UNION MILLS	125
XIII.	MOUNT VERNON	133
XIV.	THE CAPITOL AT WASHINGTON	137
XV.	LAST DAYS IN MARYLAND	143
XVI.	HOMEWARD BOUND	150
XVII.	SALT LAKE CITY	157
XVIII.	HOME AGAIN	161

SNAP NOTES.

CHAPTER I.

OVER THE RANGE.

August 17, 1891.

THE afterglow of sunset, gleaming through warm folds of purple haze overhanging the crest of Tamalpais, steals down softly and silently over rippling waves of the lovely bay, as we, a knot of kinsfolk, seat ourselves comfortably in the Oakland ferryboat, preparatory to temporarily exchanging California's matchless clime and genial fellowship for Eastern scenes and society. Later, 'twixt the hours of seven and eight, darkness crept "from the wings of night," and finds us cozily ensconced in the drawing room of a Pullman palace carriage midway in the train of fourteen cars, and forming a direct contrast to the historical pilgrims who trod westward the same route in less enviable style, in the memorable "pioneer days."

After friends, who accompany us thus far, have taken leave of the party, we start on the Eastward "tack," and ere lapsing many miles partake of a collation, plenteously provided by a thoughtful friend.

Now, watching the Marin hills slowly fading into the dim distance, with the familiar outlines of grand old Tamalpais gradually receding from view, effects a sense of lonesomeness only experienced when leaving those we love, by whom we have been always surrounded, even though absence may cover but the space of a few months. The shadow of gloom is partly dispelled by our chaperon's call to cheerfulness, with a gentle reminder that the spirit of happiness and mirth should govern the members of our party, whom I shall endeavor to introduce to my diary. We are five. Busily engaged hanging hats, wraps, etc., where they must remain for several days, is Mrs. Murphy, worthy wife of my excellent cousin, Hon. B. D. Murphy, of San Jose. Merrily humming "Mary and John," she is cheery and light-hearted as a bird, and anxious that all should be as happy as herself.

Reclining lazily on a cushioned sofa is her daughter, Miss Evalyn, who, after gracefully cutting the pages of "Under Two Flags," languidly prepares for rest. A recent student with the Madames of the Sacred Heart, I hope for interesting conversational companionship in this accomplished daughter of my respected kinsman, which hope gilds the prospect of a long journey with pleasure.

Arranging her locks before one of the many mirrors that line our boudoir, stands Miss Maud Arqués, my other cousin, a perfect "daughter of the gods, divinely tall," and lovely as an houri, her olive complexion and black hair proclaiming her one of "Spain's dark-eyed daughters."

Darting hither and thither, to and from the drawing room, the life and joy of the occasion, a "bother" yet a pleasure, is Martin Murphy, eldest son of Hon. B. D., destined for Georgetown University, whither his mother is accompanying him. Last and least is this "chield amang ye takin' notes,—and faith I'll print them!" Retiring at ten o'clock, I find to my anxiety that slumber fails to visit mine eyelids, and am wide-awake at eleven o'clock, as we are launched into Sacramento, where we linger a weary length of time. Mrs. Murphy and Miss Arques, who have not retired, are looking out upon the city and conversing with acquaintances. Sleep for me has vanished for the night, the unusual noise and motion of the cars having banished "nature's sweet restorer," leaving me awake, to the influence of thought-producing, meditative night.

August 18, Tuesday.

We climbed the Sierras during the hours of darkness, and nothing more picturesque than long snowsheds meets my glance of curiosity and interest, as I stealthily raise the curtain for a glimpse of the rugged scenery. At eight o'clock we arrive at Truckee, but must note the environs and town on our return trip, as I am too tired and unrefreshed to view it satisfactorily, in the somber gray of early morning. Steaming along the south bank of the Truckee, where romantic beauty abounds,—water rippling over rocks in frothy fretfulness, the low, craggy banks fringed with tamarack saplings and fragrant pine trees—but at these I may only glance, as breakfast is announced, and we must proceed to the dining car. During the meal we enter Reno, at nine o'clock. The dusky tribe are out in full force and glare of color, the women particularly brilliant in flashy calicoes, and heads ornamented with bright 'kerchiefs, that on Arabs might be called *tarbooshes*, or perhaps *kufiyehs*, but our more familiar and comprehensive language simply styles *bandannas*. The novel scene is especially interesting to a veritable "innocent abroad" like myself. I admire the valley outstretching from Reno, but the admiration ceases when the eye is carried to the hills, arid and bleak-looking in their covering of sagebrush. A monotonous sameness of lifeless waste characterizes the country until reaching Wadsworth, on the east bank of the Truckee, two hundred and seventy-eight miles from San Francisco. Here we delay for ten minutes, alight from the train, stroll about, and Martin tries several kodak pictures. When about reëntering the train, I meet Mr. John T. Malone, the actor, who remembered me from my convent days. He was delighted to have met the party at Sacramento, and, upon Mrs. Murphy's invitation, enters our drawing room, and entertains us most agreeably. He pointed out the "sink of the Humboldt," of which I have so often heard my father speak, in relating his pioneer experiences and vicissitudes crossing these "plains." We are pleased to have Mr. Malone's interesting companionship over this "realm of drifting sand," the Humboldt Desert, which takes a whole day to span. He recalls some incidents of my earlier acquaintance with him, amuses us with accounts and plots of different plays, and, indeed, makes us feel how "lightly falls the foot of time, that only treads on flowers." My first letter home, to dear Nellie, I post at Lovelocks, in the heart of the desert. Our next stopping-place is Humboldt, a fresh, green spot, a perfect oasis, indeed, in this dreary sand waste, and here we take our luncheon, enjoying a waiting of ten minutes. Martin, our "local artist," essayed to kodak our group, with Mr. Malone in the center.

It is now 3:30 P. M. and Winnemucca lies in sight, a larger town than I expected to see, but no more charming in appearance than others of the vast, dreary, sterile plain, that "lies like a load on the wearied eye." The name is Indian, and the cognomen of a Piute chief who was one of several who resided here during the romantic era of the West.

At four o'clock we pass through Elkon, another *desert*(ed) village of no great prominence, and I glance out with the same result, the old "bald, blear skull of the desert" still shining under glare of the sinking sun.

Battle Mountain is reached at 5:30 P. M., where Mrs. Huntsman, a former resident of San Jose, keeps a wayside hotel, which was shown to us, with the proprietress in the front yard. The place derives its name from the fact that thirty-five or more years ago was witnessed a desperate contest between white emigrants and settlers and Indians in the valleys, or river "sinks," of Reese River country, which gave the name "Battle Mountains" to the general range south of this town. And now, as we speed onward at the rate of twenty-five or more miles per hour, I peer backward, and, far as the taxed vision can stretch, I see the arid plains still, mapping a great territory, never seeming to diminish nor vary in feature,—sagebrush and sand, with occasional green spots, where cattle gather, well appreciating the dwarfed herbage on these pleasant places of this dull, desolate, sage-ridden land. My fancy wings itself with thoughts of the early travelers to the Western slope. How many times they crossed the winding Humboldt! How wearily, yet patiently, they must have breathed the hot air and alkaline dust of this trackless, treeless wilderness! Or, if its broad, flat bosom rested 'neath a mantle of snow when they were wending their way to the Western Mecca of their hopes, how irksome to the eye, how discouraging to the anxious heart, the outlook of their cherished plans!

Ere approaching Argenta, I remark herds of healthy-looking stock calmly browsing along the banks of a refreshing stream, but looking as tired of the "still solitudes of the desert" as ourselves. Argenta (silver) is a small spot not worthy of note beyond the fact that, after crossing the Humboldt River, it ushers us into the

Valley of the Palisades, a strange uprising of rocky formation on both sides of the railroad, with a swiftly-coursing creek on the south side. After emerging from the cañon and indulging in more desert land we touch Carlin, an important town of many thousand inhabitants. It is here that the Mary's Creek joins the oft-mentioned Humboldt. A brief pause, and we again bowl along towards Elko, the cattle-shipping point of the plains, whence the herds of stock are forwarded eastward. Passing several small stations we come upon Halleck, which embraces four houses on the south side of the railroad track, and Uncle Dan Murphy's large dwelling standing alone on the north side, as isolated of cheerful surroundings as is a man's life in the midst of a divided household. It is now late; we close our windows. Mr. Malone has remained in our drawing room conversing, but, midnight approaching, he and Martin have taken leave, and we retire, weary and heavy eyed.

CHAPTER II.

FROM OGDEN EAST OVER THE DENVER AND RIO GRANDE.

August 19, Wednesday.

WE were awakened this morning at half past six, at Ogden, and found breakfast waiting for us in the hotel. Mr. Malone is with us until his train starts, when we part, to continue the journey by the Denver and Rio Grande, over Burlington route, he pursuing his course by Central road, *via* Cheyenne, etc. We leave Ogden, the great railroad center, about half past eight o'clock. We are now eight hundred and thirty-three miles from San Francisco. The Weber River runs to the right of the road going east and the great craggy range of the Wasatch Mountains stands out on the left. At Ogden, in Weber County, Utah, four different railroad lines meet. The valley leading to the Jordan is a generous-sized plain under cultivation, and nearing Salt Lake City is refreshingly green and beautiful, with the bosky, bleak mountains towering cloudward to the east. Wood's Crossing and other Mormon hamlets scatter along until we reach the prophet's town, a large, flat city, with long, tree-lined, shady streets, a busy population, evidences of industry on all sides, the general air of the place having an inviting charm, indescribable in such brief notice. The houses are built principally of brick. It is the largest city I have seen since leaving San Francisco. Arriving here at 9:45 o'clock A. M., we are bounding through the valley, with its soft carpet of green alfalfa and other rich grasses, squares of grain fields lately cut, corn just in tassel, in abundance, and everything speaking with a voice of plenty.

I should judge the climate to be unexcelled, *out of California, of course.*

The rugged Wasatch Range, on our left, as we steam through, is as absolutely picturesque as the high mountains of Italy, of which we read, and deserves to be entitled the American Alps. At present these mountains are in places covered with a white limestone resembling snow, and are wildly grand beyond powers of my untraveled mind to pen paint. I marvel if human feet have ever traversed their rocky, craggy, eerie heights. The valley throughout shows the happy results of irrigation, as the sage-brush flats, by its magical means, have been metamorphosed into flourishing, healthy-looking pastures of sweet, waving grasses.

After another treat to gray sage in the Jordan Narrows, we come into Lehi, at eleven o'clock, a pretty little place within shadow of the range, on Utah Lake, an elongated body of fresh water to the south of the valley. The Utah Sugar Company are here erecting extensive buildings in the interests of their business. The valley resembles that of Salt Lake, and the towns merge into each other, the next being American Fork, situated on Deer Creek, near Mount Aspinwall, whose altitude of eleven thousand and eleven feet casts a lengthened shadow. The silver ribbon, Utah Lake, still stretches its thirty miles of weary length along the southern line of the pleasant vale within half a mile of our train. Provo, on the east bank of the lake is noteworthy for its fine woolen mills; the buildings, of stone, four stories high, attract attention. Here we alight from the cars and take our luncheon at the hotel, where we have an excellent meal, resuming our places on the train at twelve o'clock. In another few minutes we pass Springville, thence through a fruit and garden country as beautiful and fertile as human heart could desire, the effect of industry and irrigation. Utah Lake is still visible. Spanish Fork, on river of the same name, is surrounded by orchards and ornamental trees, with thriving vegetable gardens in abundance. Here Martin took a "special" photograph, a reversed observatory, minus telescope lens, and even window glass. Careering onward we enter Spanish Fork Cañon, the great gorge of the Wasatch, and come upon the Castilla Hot Springs, where hundreds of people are rusticating, presenting an enchanting scene as they saunter forth to meet our train, gayly singing or chatting, decked out in green garlands and bright flowers. Right here we are overtaken by a rainstorm, that pelts down as mercilessly as any boasted California winter showers.

Next comes in sight Red Narrows, a strange construction of abrupt declivities, rocky, yet covered with a verdant growth, which betimes disappears, leaving the crags as bald and destitute of vegetation as the worn crest of Ben Nevis, but brilliant in color of crimson chrome and other mineral elements. A laughing stream flows at the base of the cliffs, skirted by willow and shrubs, fragrant and sweet. We stop here but a few minutes, then steam onward, passing Junction a few hundred yards further, the rain continuing until we get through the cañon. We find the "Gates Ajar" of Castle Rock, and enter. The Castle rocks are of lava precipitation, as though thrown up by volcanic eruption, and present an imposing spectacle, resembling the picturesque beauty of Old World ruined castles and feudal ramparts in their beetling strength. After leaving the cliffy gorge behind us, we enter upon a particularly lime country, where kilns formed like immense beehives diversify the scenery of limerock hills covered with undersized pine trees. Especially interesting are the seams in the hillsides of variegated stone that project in tireless rows, like even sets of teeth or columns of books. About two o'clock we halt at Clear Creek to water the engine. Crossing the *Divide*, near Summit or Soldiers' Station, elevation seven thousand four hundred and sixty-five feet, we strike the snowsheds. Pleasant Valley Junction, the next station, is another dreary spot backed by barren uplands or hills, that do not even afford an imposing appearance. Pleasant *here* is a misnomer.

"Castle Gate," the great opening to the Mormon country from the East, is a novel and mysterious creation of rock into castle-like battlements of Titanic strength and magnificence, and what powerful "bulwarks to the nation" they would prove in warfare, since they solemnly withstand without injury the continuously attacking elements! Wonderful scenery, marvelous handicraft of a powerful Creator!

Price, altitude five thousand five hundred and forty-seven feet, is pleasantly located in sight of the fortlike buttes towards the west, where the strangely-formed city, abounding in prodigious buildings of nature's own construction, looms up. We are here informed that we shall be delayed three hours on account of landslides on the track a couple of miles farther. Obliged to accept the situation gracefully, we conclude to walk around, and are soon informed that we may be forced to remain all night and take dinner in this less than one-horse town, which we do about six o'clock, in a small Mormon hotel. We were waited upon by a saucy piece of humanity, who belongs, I doubt not, to the prophet's creed; and if ever she becomes "sealed" to one of the elders, the elder will be the first to wish the seal broken. The dining room is filled with flies, *hungry as ourselves.* The improvista meal is uninviting, and wholly unappetitious, but the sound fun adduced from the occasion repaid for the need of strong stomachs. I presented Maud with a *souvenir spoon* of the memorable place, to be had at *but one Price*, selected one for myself as a *chromo* for the meal, as we paid triple value for the latter, and I conclude that *Price* is properly named.

Martin is amusing himself with the kodak,

seeing which a woman emerges from a wretched-looking dwelling and eagerly asks, "Takin' picters?" "Our artist," not being certain of success, modestly stammers an answer in the affirmative, and the simple creature instantly starts for her house, immediately returning with an infant, which she wished to have photographed. Martin was caught, but gracefully acceded to her request, and kindly kodaked the little Mormon, whereupon she anxiously asked if she might see the "likeness," and, "How much is the *pay?*" He explained the impracticability of the former, and *generously waived all claim to the latter*, cheerfully assuring the poor woman that *when* he succeeded in perfecting the little beauty's picture he would send it to her. She congratulated him upon the pleasure of having taken the virgin photo of the small stranger, and, in her delight, they forgot all about names, addresses, etc., so the doting mother will long wait for the "picter" of her darling, that can never come.

After eight hours' delay they told us the sand drift had been removed, and we could gladly continue our journey. We retired, and soon the city of several hundred Mormons and *three Gentiles* was far behind. During the night we traveled rapidly, and, fortunately, crossed the pathless tracks of the Colorado Desert without knowing it, and this, Thursday morning, we awake to find ourselves in Colorado, August 20, with small chances for breakfast. The first station I note is De Beque, a small settlement on the sand flat through which the railway runs. We observe the river flowing parallel with the railroad, a large, wildly turbulent, muddy stream. The scenery is tame and uninteresting hereabout, except for peculiar bluffs of clay studded with rock that rise on either side in somewhat fantastic formation. The diminutive hamlets dotting the route are unworthy of comment, save for their lonely locations. Again, alfalfa-clad meadows please the eye for a long stretch, to Rifle, a railroad village of no significance, and on until the oft-repeated scene becomes tiresome. At ten o'clock we stop at Newcastle for water. It is a hamlet, built between craggy mountains, steep and rugged, garnished only with wild, straggling, stunted pines. Bowling along through the rocky cañon we come upon Glenwood and Glenwood Springs, most romantically situated on the banks of the royal Grand, a dark, strong, shallow stream, at times suggesting the Russian River, of Sonoma County, California, so familiar to us all. The scenery is here wild and primeval, at times weird, but always picturesque. The cliffs rise from the river bed hundreds of feet heavenward, are covered with loose rock kept from shifting into the river by dwarfed pines and roots of other stunted trees. The walls of bare brown rock at times surprise and fill the soul with awe and wonder.

The Glenwood Springs are the resort for Eastern people who spend the summer here; particularly is it a Mecca for consumptives. Many of their tents and cabins are scattered along the railroad line, suggesting the comfort here found by these elsewhere hopeless invalids. It is a lovely, lonely spot. The hotel, of brown Colorado stone, is a grand structure, and the pretty lakelet and sparkling fountain most charmingly cheery and inviting. The country hereabouts is indeed mountainous, looking tumbled and disordered. Hastening onward, we pass through three tunnels, and now the rocky walls take a shelving character, and rise in strength and effect until one ceases to marvel at their towering heights, and we realize at last that we are indeed in the heart of the Rocky Mountains. Here I am particularly surprised at the massive grandeur of the gorge, wholly unlike anything yet seen. We emerge into a broader vale, through the center, tracing the same yellow stream coursing onward through the cañon. The near mountains, in their red cinnabar skin, have a magnetic attraction for me. It is now half past eleven, yet we have not broken fast, and all are beginning to sympathize in the hunger of the ill-fated Donner party of 1846. Having spanned some distance, and reached more sage land, I note the mountains lowering in stature, and soft, fleecy clouds hang in the sky, screening us from the garish glare of piercing sunlight. A post marked "Eagle" calls my attention, and, glancing out, I mark the green bit of landscape lit up by the crystal glitter of the stream. Giving our thirsty engine a drink, we cross the river and leave it in the distance. The conductor informs me that the ravine—from the above-mentioned post—is called Eagle River Valley. The views along the banks and rock towers are similar to those of the Rio Grande. My companions and self are on the platform enjoying the "sights" that are seen and carried away like dissolving views. We reach the Rio Grande Hotel at one o'clock P. M., and have a good, comfortable breakfast and lunch combined. Girls wait upon us, in a polite manner, and are neat as rosebuds. Picturesque log cabins for consumptives dot the banks of the stream and railroad line again, looking cozy and comfortable, so peculiarly adapted as buildings to this wild region. The mountains to their dizzy peaks are densely *clothed with fir* and pine, scant of foliage, and showing signs in many places of having been visited at a recent date by fire. Panda, another diminutive sign, passes us on to a small tunnel, which wafts my thoughts back to San Rafael. A quiet, charming little fertile valley runs north from this spot, which is lost to the eye in the darksome depths of the rugged Rockies. Wild flowers cheer the wayside with their bright presence, and are like the low, soft voices of cherished friends calling us down from contemplation of those tremendous boulders and bluffs that have been holding our hearts in awe and admiration.

Along here we enter a tunnel so many feet in length that it takes four minutes to pass through; then comes Tennessee Pass tunnel, which is noted by Mrs. Murphy as I slept, the drowsy influence having possessed me for the first time. I awake with a chill, and, noting the altitude, am physically aware that the raw air is due to the unmelted snow on the sculpturesque chain of the Rockies surrounding us, the first snow we have seen. A small hamlet, Barnetts, rapidly followed by Riverside, and we glide through pleasant plains, with the Denver and Rio Grande Narrow Gauge on our left. The rocks are less precipitous and imposing.

Before us spread vast fields of potatoes and grain, with a clear, limpid stream flowing through them. In one field hay cutting had begun. The country now resembles California, since crossing the range. The tortuous Marshall Pass is entrancing in its fear-inspiring grandeur. At 5:30 P. M. we are brought into Salida, and dinner announced, of which we partake *con gusto*. "Monte Christo Hotel" belongs to the Rio Grande Company, and the meal was the best we have had since leaving California, even before "the buffet went on with Malone," at Ogden.

Walking around for a few minutes, Maud and I swell our spoon collection, and all re-enter the train, after a last glance at the Swiss style and setting of the hotel in the midst of created beauty. We hear a puff and a screech and away we go, leaving Salida, on the Arkansas, beautifully embedded in leafy solitudes. My girl cousins and self are seated upon the platform and steps to view the country, and I note Texas Creek as one of the stations. We are speeding, they say, at the rate of twenty-five miles per hour, and almost repeating the scenery of the Rio Grande in Texas Creek Cañon. We arrive at a place lettered "SALOON," *whatever that means*, six miles from the Royal Gorge of the Arkansas, which we are anxiously waiting to behold. The sable wings of night are silently folding, yet we hope to view the gorgelike storied "Melrose" by moonlight. The river is on our right, wild and wide, seething, tumbling over broken rocks, with fantastic shadows lurking o'er its troubled bosom, whilst it roars in hollow tones to the echo of the winding abyssmal chasm. Cañon City, a prettilyset place of several thousand inhabitants, on the Arkansas, backed by mountains, is happily a breathing-place after the suppressed emotion inspired by the most sublimely grand vista in the scenic history of wonderful Colorado. The magnificent bluffs of the Royal Gorge loom skyward three thousand feet, some of them overhanging the train, rendering the wild landscape charmingly fascinating in its awful danger.

Silence falls upon the trio; awe is expressed in every feature; and I look up with a sense of devotion, picturing the sky reaching down to kiss the ambitious brows of the lofty cliffs, leaving breath thereon in form of curling clouds. These almost star-high reaching ramparts of God's solid masonry climb higher and higher, each more imposing in imperial supremacy than the last, on either side of the passageway through which the river and our iron horse race.

As we, in tremorous fear, continue to gaze

upward, in all the dignity of silence, at God's matchless work, the night clouds lower, but another bend in the high-walled cañon shows the moon bursting in brilliant effulgence of shimmering silver upon the sinuous river, over which is flung, in clearly mirrored outlines, branches and limbs of poplar, willow, and cottonwood, making a weird picture for black and white effect.

We enter the drawing room, and I sit by the window watching all the moon reveals. I pleasurably note the rippling, dimpling, purling river running beside us, then curving away to hide amid trees and shrubbery, the moon rays glittering upon its bosom, and casting smiling beams upon rock and tree and stream alike, yet received differently by each.. Mr. and Mrs. C., of Philadelphia, are spending the evening with us, in our drawing room. At nine o'clock P. M. we draw up at Pueblo, an important city, on the Arkansas River also, receiving its name from the fact that it remains on the site of an old Mexican *pueblo*, which means town. The tourist, from the train, observes for the most prominent feature an elegant hotel of stone, built at enormous cost, standing at the depot, presenting a substantial appearance. At one gable end is a tall tower, embracing a clock. The street cars run over an elevated bridge spanning the railroad near the hotel and adding to its business effect. The location of the city, in the heart of such a rich State, with so many natural advantages, cannot fail to speed its rapid progress towards becoming the "leading manufacturing center between the Missouri River and Pacific Coast." Gliding slowly on, the dark, deep waters of the river course through the city, and the number of railroad tracks prove the importance of Pueblo's position as a commercial mart. Scudding away we come to Colorado Springs, a healthful, fashionable, and romantic resort. Our Philadelphia acquaintances leave us here, and I peer out for a view of the surroundings, but, like the Garden of the Gods, which misty half-light prevented a view of, now this lovely spot too is obscured, yet I succeed in catching a glimpse of a Monte Christan scene on the mountain ledge west of the town, where electric lights play fantastic pranks with stray moonbeams. They tell me it is Colorado Springs Hotel, a beautiful and popular resort. It is now 11:30 o'clock P. M. We are heading for Denver, and are about to retire, to allow weary nature her just repose.

CHAPTER III.

FROM DENVER TO DETROIT.

August 21, Friday.

WE were called early this morning, as our train steamed into Denver and, rising immediately, dressed quickly, leaving our Pullman sleeper, "Estrella," with fond farewell and mental gratitude for its very comfortable conveyance of us so far. We take a carriage and drive to the "Windsor," a fine house, conducted on the English plan, have breakfast, and come to our rooms to prepare for an outing. The morning is lovely, balmy, and fresh, the air keen and invigorating. We boarded the cable car, and rode the length of Larimer Street and back, took transfers to Sixteenth Street, the most superb and interesting thoroughfare in Denver, walled on both sides with immense stone and brick business buildings, and farther out residences of wealthy people fill the sight, green lawns and pretty gardens please, and everything presents a heavy, massive appearance, owing, I suppose, to the stone, to which I am, as a Californian, unaccustomed. It began raining soon after we started out, and has continued all day. Returning for our lunch, and to write some letters and telegrams, at three o'clock we ordered a carriage and drove all around the phenomenal city, of over one hundred thousand inhabitants, thence up "Castle Hill," where everything to be shown we saw. The residences and homes of merchants, bankers, cattle kings and mine owners, ex-governors, senators, and other noted individuals, are remarkably elegant. The house of Senator Tabor is a superb structure, and that of Mr. Porter, the greatest cattle king of Colorado, is the finest in the city, the interior decorations alone having cost a comfortable fortune. The stone State house, uncompleted, is being erected, at a cost of $3,000,000, and promises to be superior to any public building in the great West. In driving about we pass by the St. Mary's Academy for young ladies, conducted by the Sisters of Loretta, a large, commodious brick building. We make some purchases, commemorative of our visit, and return to the Windsor. Dine at six, and at half past eight take the train for Omaha, *en route* for Chicago.

Mrs. Murphy secured the "Garda" on the vestibule sleeper of the Burlington route, and we are again very comfortably situated, and happy as heretofore. The prime adventure of the drawing room was experienced by Mrs. Murphy, but her own diary must furnish the details. After we retired, I experienced extreme cold, and remembered, with a longing heart, my sealskin coat, over a thousand miles away. With the first streaks of dawn we were aroused for breakfast, and partook of it in the "diner," reaching Holdridge during the meal. We are now traveling over Nebraska, a thrifty-looking and productive country, under cultivation as far as the eye is unforbidden by distance to go. Axtell, Heartwell, and other small, unimportant places are rapidly viewed as we steam through a fine farming and grazing territory. The air is chilly, but the day is bright and sunny.

Upon nearing Hastings I inquire about the Platte River. A gentleman furnishes the information that it is farther south, on the Atchison, Topeka, and Santa Fe route, whereat I am disappointed, being deprived of going over part of the pioneers' trail, of which I have so often heard my dear ones speak. The broad fields are teeming "rich with golden grain." Farmhouses, environed by orchards and small flower gardens and vegetable plots, dot the vast expanse, relieving the eye of grain and corn views. At Fairmount we lunch in dining car

"Lincoln," and enjoy both the occasion and repast. Nothing noteworthy in sight.

The towns resemble California rural districts; the houses are all built of wood, like ours, and the fencing is all wire. Stock appear in limited number, but look fat and well. These vast plains, flat as a slate, replete with the result of farmers' industry and pluck, were like the Nevada sweep of sage land when our sturdy pioneers of '44 wended their way westward. The majority of those pioneers have passed to their last resting station, after having surmounted the wearisome mountains of life's difficulties, and patiently trod the monotonous plains of existence, meekly obedient to the will of our Heavenly Father, and gratefully responsive when his voice summoned their tired feet to rest and their wandering hearts home, and these prairies are ateem with the result of work and wealth. At Lincoln, Neb., we halted about two o'clock, and had twenty-five minutes to walk around. Cousin Maud, as usual, made a raid on the fruit man, and, to our surprise, was informed that miserable pears were four for twenty-five cents, whereas in California we would fling the same kind of fruit away. Think of selling a half-spoiled pear for six and one-fourth cents, bananas (half black and all soft) four for a quarter, and five peaches at the same rate. Verily, one must travel to learn the value of what we depreciate, even scorn, at home. If this is not the "corn-cracker State," it ought to be, we see such profusions of it growing, and what we had at table was excellent.

Ashland is green and pretty; the pastures feed fine cattle, and the vernal spring of our peerless State is not more beautiful than the country I here behold. We cross a broad, sandy-bottomed river, which just above us is spanned by a long bridge, and its low banks are self-edged with trees and undergrowth. Upon consulting my map I find that it is the oft-heard-of Platte. The gentleman who blighted my hopes as to its location was wrong. Numerous herds of contented cattle are scattered over the verdant flat, presenting a happy picture. The country of the Platte is indeed "green fields and pastures new." How my heart yearns for the impossible privilege of conversing upon these scenes with my late father, and comparing notes with his experiences! The hay, I notice, is stacked in small pineapple shape, and looks odd to Californians.

Our matron has amused herself playing *Solitaire* nearly all day *a la* Mr. Ballou, of Mark Twain's sagebrush days. Cousin Evie has slept most of the time, in an easy posture, which I am sure she enjoys. Cousin Maude talked, read "Lost in New York," bought fruit, and performed her ablutions about every half hour in hopes of transferring as little real estate as possible from Nebraska.

I snapped off these straggling notes, and watched the scenery. At half past three in the afternoon we heard "Omaha!" called, and I strained my eyes to obtain a full view of the city, and Council Bluffs, with its world of memories to the pioneers. Our stay of half an hour's duration was employed by our party in walking around, viewing the surroundings for mental storing, eating popcorn—Maud's treat, of course—and talking over our experiences thus far. At 4:15 o'clock we respond to the order, "All aboard!" and are soon steaming rapidly along the banks of the Missouri, on the western border of the State of Iowa. The vicinity is the scene so cherished by our pioneers, whence they date the beginning of their westward pilgrimage, "Crossing the Missouri River at Council Bluffs on the 3d of May, 1844," etc., and now my memory, charged with long recitals of their vicissitudes, is overpowered by a sea of emotion, and I cannot restrain the tears that well up, to the sweet relief of my heart. Have just passed by Plattsmouth Station, and a few minutes brings us to the lengthy bridge across the Missouri's broad bosom, which bridge, I am told, is half a mile long. As I gaze back upon the scene, it is one of interest and beauty, the valley thickly set with natural trees and trailing brush, the waters of the wide river gleaming through them like flecks of silver, in the rich flush of the setting sun. The meadow lands are flourishing and freshly springlike, dotted with cattle, lazy and fat. Pacific Junction is the first station that delays us a length of time. It is here the trains for the Pacific meet, from Missouri and the East The next cozy hamlet is Glenwood, a sweet little place, full of romantic situations.

Creston, a larger town, was gained about 8:30 P. M., and is brightly attractive at night in the garish glare of gas and electric lights. We retire, weary indeed, and, after broken snatches of sleep, unrefreshing, to say the least, are aroused at 7 o'clock A. M., Sunday, August 23, to dress for breakfast, in the expectation of reaching Chicago on time. The suburbs of the metropolis, as we approach, are alluring in their peace-filled beauty and restfulness, but I am eager to enter "the Windy City," and can only glance at these introductory charms to it. At 8 o'clock we reach the depot, secure a conveyance, and are rattled through the sloppy streets to the "Auditorium," an elegant hotel overlooking

Lake Michigan. The building is ten stories high, with a tower ten tiers higher, from which a bird's-eye view of the whole city may be obtained. The view from our window, in the seventh story, is truly interesting. The great blue lake stretches its heaving bosom of sixty miles before my unaccustomed vision, and its majestic length of three hundred and fifty miles sweeps beyond sight. As I stand by the window, viewing with curiosity and wonder the largest lake it has been my fortune to see, I note the steamboats plying to and fro over its rippling surface, landing passengers almost "within a stone's throw" of our location, then the ten railroad tracks parallel with the sweep of green-swards seamed with paths, and next the clean, broad, smooth boulevard called Michigan Avenue.

After refreshing our appearances, a most necessary and satisfactory obligation, we descend to our dinner in the French restaurant, on the first floor, the hotel being one of those conducted on the European plan. After dinner, procuring a carriage with "a character" for a coachman, we drive to the parks, World's Fair grounds, *via* the cleanly boulevard, which our driver innocently styles "the bully-yard." Like Denver's soft treat, it began raining soon after we started out and has kept continually pouring; twice we sought shelter in stables awaiting the abatement of the rainstorm. The park has some excellent specimens of landscape gardening, particularly noticeable a "World's Fair Globe" surmounting a green knoll, the water being represented in *Echeverias Metalica* and the continents by the red *Coleus*. Probably the novel arrangement, measuring several feet in diameter, has been constructed of wire filled in with earth, the plants sown on the outside, the whole being ingeniously designed. Returning we seek the seclusion which our boudoirs grant, and soon retire to sleep soundly.

Monday, August 24.

After our matin meal, Martin, Maud, and myself go out shopping, and to see the city that pork and pluck have made famous. We see none of the former. Mrs. Murphy is quite ill, so we do not remain away longer than to purchase a few souvenirs, beautiful spoons being our most valuable collection. During the afternoon I remain with Mrs. M., while my cousins go out and around, and in the evening to the theater. I decline attending amusements with them during my season of wearing mourning, and retire at midnight to enjoy balmy sleep.

Tuesday, August 25.

Rose this morning at seven o'clock, breakfasted at ten, thereafter packed our trunks for Boston. I wrote letters to some friends in New England, acquainting them with the likelihood of my presence in the vicinity of their abiding places. Mrs. Murphy went with me to Father D. J. Riordan's residence, whose address had been kindly furnished me by His Grace Archbishop Riordan prior to my departure from California.

With a stubborn coachman and limited time we are deprived of seeing other friends and the pleasure of visiting the cathedral built by the late Bishop Thomas Foley, which I was desirous of inspecting. We return to dine at the hotel and prepare for the train, which leaves at 3:10 P. M., and we are "on time" at the busy depot, of which we take farewell without regret. Now, at 3:30 o'clock, we are flying on the wings of steam along the shore of the beautiful blue lake, leaving the tall buildings of the phœnix-like city in the distance, getting glimpses of small towns along the route, but moving too rapidly to be able to read the names on the stations. At 5:10 we rush into Michigan City, in the "Hoosier" State, Indiana. Have remarked the forests of small trees growing thickly, and meadow lands whence timber has been removed look rich and thrifty under cultivation, but, like similar spots in California, have many tree stumps ungrubbed in their midst.

Michigan City is a large, enterprising place, with a generous supply of natural trees and tall church spires. I recognize the Catholic edifice, with its gilded cross surmounting the tower. We now occupy the drawing rooms of the "Tidal Wave" coach, of Michigan Central. The almost dense forests of young growth obscure the view on either side of the railroad, and the country, Michigan, we are traversing is full of health-giving properties and extensive agricultural advantages. Timber resembling our lofty redwood attracts my fancy, but I believe it is a species of fir. A little station is marked Averys, in the heart of enviable surroundings as far as created beauty goes, thence another forest, followed by homes of farmers snug in sweet content, with orchards fruit laden and graceful corn fields. We have just been regaled by sight of a lovely, grassy-edged lake, whose breast palpitates beneath a fragrant load of water lilies, lazy and lolling as those of the Nile, but we are swept onward ere the vision is fully satisfied. At 5:45 we "slow up" at Niles, on the banks of the St. Josephs River, a romantic looking stream, and are delayed a few minutes. A boy opens our drawing room unceremoniously, and presents each lady with an exquisite little bouquet, "Compliments of Chief Engineer's Office, Niagara Falls Route," of Michigan Central.

Well launched on the "Tidal Wave," skimming over the southern portion of the State, I mark verdurous forest and grove and silvery streams peeping through the bushes, then "running away," as though affrighted by the snort of the iron steed, as he madly dashes past. Foliaged trees again over numberless acres. Verily Michigan is a richly wooded State. Having coursed over a fine country, we reach Ostemo at 6:55, a small place of no particular distinction, and, darkness suddenly wafting downwards, our gas is lit, and we shall soon——pardon me for using a nautical phrase—"turn in."

About seven o'clock we enter Kalamazoo, a city I have often heard of. A church is prominent near the railroad track. Its two very lofty spires, with plain Roman crosses, show up conspicuously as we approach. The city is large and flourishing, with an outlook of assured prosperity. The river and its bridge are valuable adjuncts to its features. Continuing onward we sight Jackson, another large, important city, and then Ann Arbor, patronized by Californians for the college of law it maintains. Nearing Detroit, our luggage had to be checked or marked before crossing the river into Ontario, Canada, across which we must run to Niagara. At ten o'clock P. M. we steam away from Ypsilanti to the Detroit. We reach Detroit City late, and I am suggesting to Mrs. Murphy to "stop off" here for the night and obtain a view of the city, call upon Bishop John Foley, and resume our journey to-morrow evening, but she thinks otherwise, so we retire to rest, which we all need, and the confusion and noise crossing the river is anything but conducive to peaceful slumber.

CHAPTER IV.

A VISIT TO NIAGARA.

August 26, Wednesday.

AT seven o'clock we are called up at Falls View to see Niagara. The vast sweep of waters to the falls is to me more surprising than the falls themselves, inasmuch as I had never seen pictures of them from the point whence we now inspect them, and they do not impress me with their enormity. In a few minutes we cross the great Cantilever Bridge, nine hundred and ten feet long, and are at Niagara. We register at the Cataract House for the day, taking an early breakfast, then secure a three-seated conveyance, and ride to the different points of interest. Driving over a common rough country road of some distance, the first scene visited is Whirlpool Rapids, where we pause, overawed at the grand spectacle, the fierce, wild, angry-looking waters rushing madly downwards, throwing up foam in feathery flecks as it dashes over the crags that form the rude bed of the river. The force of the water flow here is tremendous, yet it must be borne in mind that the supply, from four great lakes, compressed in the width of three hundred feet, rushes frantically onward at the rate, I believe, of twenty-seven miles an hour. We had our photographs taken at this place. I ordered mine to be sent home, that the loved ones may see how I am enjoying the, to me, new wonders of God's footstool. Ascending the bank by the ingeniously-constructed elevator, we purchase some souvenirs, arraquettes, etc., etc., and drive to the great whirlpool, which is four hundred feet deep, and a marvel in itself. The swirling green waters make one dizzy to watch and wonder at. It was here that Captain Webb was last seen alive, and it is here that so many have attempted the dangerous feat of swimming across. Six men and one woman have succeeded, wearing cork jackets, and one in a lifeboat, the daring female performing the feat in a barrel. The day is beautiful, sunny, and warm—in truth, the brightest we have had since leaving Nevada. Wandering around I stray toward the stairway above the great whirlpool, and the outlet, and count sixteen hundred and sixteen steps, wearisome to look at, and a task of importance to double. The view from a pathway on the hillside, suggesting fearful power, is occasion for reflection on my own nothingness, and from this sublime scene my thoughts go back to history, to the humble Jesuit missionary of the Indians, Fr. Hennepin, whose features were the first belonging to white man reflected in these turbulent waters, as far back as 1678.

Entering another bazaar to inspect curios, of which there is an infinity, we select a few, and, taking our carriage again, return to the Cataract Hotel, two miles distant, for our lunch. The property in the vicinity of the whirlpool, on the American side, belongs to the De Veaux Military Academy, which solemn-looking stone structure, covered with ivy, we pass on our way from the bazaar. Niagara City boasts a population of seven thousand, but I have remarked very few fine-looking homes, and the houses are mostly scattering and poor. The only impressions, of course, are effected by the river and falls. The city, from my humble idea of progress, is far behind the age, considering that trains enter it every half hour, bearing excursionists by the hundred, who fill the streets, marching along with lunch baskets, but are lost amid the great wonders, to reappear when their trains return. The beautifully located city grows slowly.

Finding that it is only eleven o'clock, we conclude to cross the new suspension bridge (one thousand two hundred and sixty-eight feet long), "designed for foot passengers and carriages," and enter Canada, to view magnificent Niagara from the heights above Victoria Park. Reaching the Canadian shore, we pass the "Clifton House," a beautiful hotel, with broad porches garnished with vines, palms, and potted plants, and drive through Queen Victoria's Park, a fine lawn-covered sunny slope, whence we view in silence the great world wonder of American scenery. The day is lovely indeed, and everything conducive to the fullest enjoyment of the marvelous grandeur of the scene. We spin along the ridge to "Clark's Burning Springs," a mystery in themselves.

Entering the observatory building, we are conducted to a semi-dark room. From the center of the floor projects a pipe about two and a half feet high, connected with the Burning Spring below, and to the top of this pipe the attendant touched a lighting match, when the gas instantly burst into a soft blaze, and to it he applied a piece of newspaper, which ignited, yet the heat was not so intense that the hand could not be passed rapidly through it without burning. The keeper gave us each a drink of the water from the mineral spring connected with it. Upon asking for a result of the analysis, we were informed that it contains principally sulphur, iron, and magnesia, and my own imagination supplied stale eggs. The burning springs were discovered over a century ago, by Indians building a camp fire, and it is said that they were quickly dispersed by fright when the gas ignited and remained burning, they deeming the place haunted by evil spirits. For a great number of years the story was known only by tradition, and the spot lost sight of, until located by the present managers. Ascending to the observatory surmounting the building, I looked long and interestedly at the Niagara lake or river as it appears sullenly in the distance above the falls, the water flowing smooth and glossy in the shining sunlight, but becoming rough and foamy as it approaches the vast chasm, precipitating itself one hundred and sixty-four feet, making its fall resound to a great distance. The Iroquois language is indeed concise, for its simple word "Niagara" expresses "mighty, wonderful, thundering water." My attention, riveted in devout admiration and amazement, cannot be directed elsewhere. Turn as I may, the eye of interest reverts to the fleecy, misty, soft, eternal flow of the magnificent waters. Up on the Ontario commons stands an imposing gray stone convent, but I could not learn what order of nuns conducts it.

Ere descending from the observatory I kiss my hand to Canada, because it held the early married lives of my dear parents, and, next to California, had sweetest memories and most interest for them. As we recross the bridge, the little steamer *Maid of the Mist* is making her pleasure trips between the American and Canadian landings, and, under the spray and rainbow tinting, looks phantom-like and lovely. Prospect Park, on American side, is smaller than Victoria, but wooded and beautiful. On our way back to the hotel is shown the vessel in which the Amazon made the swim of the whirlpool. It is a long barrel, smaller at one end, with opening in the side. Reaching the "Cataract" we lunch at noon, after which Mrs. Murphy retires to her room, and we, the rest of the sight-seers, walk up to the "Cave of the Winds." I am troubled with a cold, and cannot descend, but the others do, and present a most comical appearance "rigged out" in the oil clothing furnished by the keepers. Those desirous of making the descent, upon payment of twenty-five cents each, are conducted to a dressing room, where every article of clothing is exchanged for those of oil. A tin box is also furnished, into which are placed the coin, jewelry, and other valuables, and its numbered key is hung around the neck of the owner, while the box is stored in the safe of the office. Equipped for the dangerous experiment, the comical brigade present themselves at the head of the slippery steps, and are immediately taken in charge by guides, who convey them to the cave under the Great Fall. The sensation was certainly novel. The superintendent awarded them certificates for having succeeded in making the thrilling plunge to the cave.

During their stay below I wandered around alone, visiting Luna Island and other pretty points of richly wooded grounds, strolled along the path in the woods, where numberless tourists were enjoying the day, back to the foot-bridge across the cataracts to the town, through which I leisurely sauntered, making a few purchases, thence to the hotel, and, gaining our boudoir, enjoyed a rest until nearly train-time. Summoning a servant, Mrs. Murphy ordered a carriage for our conveyance to the depot, which we reached at 5:30 o'clock P. M., where we took the New York Central train for Buffalo, but, unfortunately, boarded a local, and came near missing it, bag and baggage. Our through tickets are not recognized on the local, and we are obliged to purchase tickets to Buffalo. The car is very much crowded, and the accommodations inferior. From Niagara to Lockport is a sea of orchards as we run across the State of New York.

I take particular notice of the country on account of its distance from California, until we swing into Buffalo. Upon reaching the city of Mr. Cleveland's early political triumphs our party is thrown into dire confusion by the conductor's order that "all passengers must leave the train; it goes no further." Picture our dismay, and you will pardon our sympathy with Mark Twain's party lost in the snow, whose deathbed resolutions went for nought, for here we are, among strangers, not destined for Buffalo, but Boston. We look at each other reproachfully. Who is to blame? Martin is treated to a hasty "round up" by his mother for not having obtained the required information respecting the trains. Evie is diligently plying the question, "Where am I going?" to which repeated query the conductor impatiently replies, "How do *I* know?" Mrs. M. is collecting valises, hand bags, etc., and trying to convey them all at once from the car. In the crowd Maud has disappeared, and I am looking on, waiting for the reunion, for verily I say unto you, the California party has stampeded. Finally, with the dispersing of the throng of passengers, Maud is recovered, Mrs. Murphy has been relieved of the "**grip sacks**," Evie has discovered her latitude, for Martin has adjusted matters by having our tickets examined, resulting in the knowledge gained that the through train will arrive in a few minutes, so our spirits are again serene. I marvel at the fine city, having often heard my father speak of Buffalo as little more than a trading post in the days of the Murphy exodus from Canada. It now stretches along the Niagara River and is a great, populous city, of much importance and wealth. I remark the cathedral, I suppose, with three domes or towers topped with crosses, on our left. We take the sleeper of the Wagner vestibule, and are now, at 7 o'clock, slowly leaving Buffalo in the background, and again the simple charms of country life and well-tilled lands greet the vision.

After leaving Buffalo I eagerly caught a hurried glimpse of the placid waters of Lake Erie, to the southeast of us, and its little steamers plying their calling over its shining tide. I revive my earliest recollections of history, and recall Perry's victory with a feeling of rapture. How much more would we all enjoy this trip were any one of us posted on the names and histories of the places we see. Perhaps the scenes of cruel battles during our lamentable rebellion are skipped by as unnoticed as a stray house or a watering tank, whereas devout interest in our land would attract attention to the spot were it known, and a pious thought and prayer might be entertained for the memory of those who wore so bravely the "blue and the gray." The country is so freshly green. When *do* they have summer, dry and parched, in the East? In the gloaming we enter Batavia, on a river running southward. It is prettily located, and a neat parterre, artistically designed, marks the station, the word "Batavia" being imbedded in the lawn in white stone, which is unique and pretty. Batavia is a pretentious-looking town, with a well-filled cemetery, bordering on the railroad line. About half past eight o'clock we "pull in" to Rochester for supper, where my companions alight, but I feel too fatigued and prefer resting to eating. Glancing out I regret that darkness intervenes and prevents observation of a city I would like to see. Retired at eleven o'clock very travel tired. We occupied berths on the train in the general passenger car for the first time, and found it very inconvenient, not being accustomed to it. The upper berth is particularly low on these Boston and Albany cars, hence unpleasant for those in the lower couches. It would have been comfortable enough, however, had we not known "better days" in the drawing rooms of the Pullman and other wheeled palaces.

Thursday, August 27.

I awoke early, and, peeping out, as we stopped I read "Pittsfield," and knew I was in Massachusetts. Passing onward reached Westfield, thence Springfield, where we had our breakfast, warm and palatably served. Springfield is a beautiful city on the Connecticut River, which runs directly through it. After ten minutes' delay for the meal we are again swiftly spinning by small stations, hamlets, and important cities on our course to Boston. Massachusetts looks much like verduous Iowa and Michigan, but *so rocky!* The gray stone croppings recall places in California through northern Sonoma. The grass is emerald in hue, but the soil is not at all rich looking; the tree foliage and shrubbery are unfamiliar to me, yet pretty. I expected to see every house east of the Rockies built of stone or brick, and only found them to great extent in Denver as yet, also Chicago, which city is never a laggard in the march of improvement and progress.

We have just gained, with a short stop, Palmer, a conspicuous and not unimportant city. A mile or two further east, as I glance to our right, or south of the train, I mentally photograph a valley that is decidedly Californian in character, particularly Marin County, and, as I am so distant from the golden slope, I may be pardoned for loving the State which reproduces some of the well-known features of my own. West Warden is beautifully set between laughing streams that break and ripple over rocks, chattering in innocent noise like a bevy of merry children as they run. It has been raining since we left Springfield. No wonder that the grass is green and soft, under so much moisture. We glide by Brookfield with only time to glance at it and admire its velvety covering of beauteous lawns and shining rills and lakelets, many of them surfaced with blooming white water lilies. There are many people on the train bound for Boston who seem to have been somewhere West. Small stations, such as South Spencer, are seen and gone, barely giving time to snatch the name on memory's tablet. I can understand how easily the waters of these many streams were utilized for millwork before steam came into common use. Many mill dams suggest it. They are very picturesque. The only near hills I have seen are the Berkshire, in this State, and they resemble our own. Rochdale, on a pretty creek or, maybe, river, is a small town with few houses. The stone fences are like those in Sonoma, on the road to Napa.

About nine o'clock we reach Worcester, a city of considerable importance, with large factory interests and business buildings. The depot is an extensive affair, and the large two-steepled Catholic Church of the Jesuits, on the hill, is a prominent ornament to the town, and handsome monument to the energy and zeal of the order. Worcester is the birthplace of our noble old American historian, Bancroft. I turn my attention back to a knoll surrounded by greenswards and scattering ornamental trees, upon which stands a long gray stone building, resembling our Napa Insane Asylum. It is handsomely located, and an imposing structure.*

---

* I have since been told that it *is* the Worcester Insane Asylum.

CHAPTER V.

THE CITY OF BOSTON.

WE are nearing Boston, the baggage checkman having arrived on the scene to relieve us of the responsibility of our baggage. I learn that it is an hour's ride from Worcester to Boston. As we approach the "Athens of America," we pass near Lake Cohitchuate, which supplies the metropolis with water, a placid sheet with many small craft floating on its glassy surface. About ten o'clock we find ourselves in the "city of culture," when a cab manager at once calls a carriage for our use, adjusts the price, and gives the order to the "Hotel Vendome," thus preventing confusion to strangers or anxiety about luggage. The "Vendome," on Commonwealth Avenue, facing part of The Commons, is a very elegant white marble building, about six stories high, and covering the major part of a square The views are delightful from every side, the Charles River being one of them. It is raining here, and anything but warm, "as *we* know it." Re-

freshing ourselves, we take lunch (the hotel is
not on the European plan), and then order a
carriage for a drive to Bunker Hill Monument,
which we enjoy to the fullest. Mrs. Murphy
remained in the office, selecting souvenir
spoons, specimens of which she presented to
each of us, and the rest of the party climbed
to the summit of the tower, two hundred and
ninety-four steps, and were well wearied with
the unusual exercise. We walked around,
read the inscriptions on the slabs that mark
the walls of the old redoubt and Prescott's
statue, all of which were exceedingly interesting and historical.

Reëntering our carriage, we drive around
the strangely-planned city, which is more intricate than we could have imagined. We call
at a dry goods store, and are conveyed to its
upper stories by an elevator. The sellers of
goods are all women and young girls, the latter being the noisiest and most "slangy" lot
I ever listened to. A longer jaunt around
town, and finally home, where I found a
friend's note and card awaiting me. We dined
at 6:30 P. M. in a spacious, well-filled dining
hall, and the meal was elegantly served and
most inviting. The waiters throughout the
hotel are of the dark race, and they know their
business perfectly. My companions all at-

tended the Globe Theater, and, with a friend, I walked to the Charles River Bridge, made famous by Longfellow's song, "The Bridge," and we stood there for a few minutes watching the tide and the "tall church towers." It was very beautiful, the waters sparkling under a thousand lights, the mist overhanging the quiet city rendering the sky-piercing spires phantom-like and stately. The theater party returned at half past ten.

Friday, August 28.

I arose, donned my attire early, and wrote several letters. My friend Dr. F., of Worcester, kindly sent a message to the effect that he would come around between eight and nine to take us to Cambridge. He was on time, but, as my cousins had not yet appeared, I accepted his invitation to visit the Notre Dame Convent, of which my California Alma Mater is a branch, to meet his sister, also to see the Cathedral of Holy Cross, Immaculate Conception Church of the Jesuits, who also own and conduct Boston College, adjoining the edifice. It rained incessantly. I have learned how to use an umbrella since leaving California. The rain becoming stormy, we called a cab, and comfortably drove about to the places of interest, the State House, with its gilded dome, Boston Commons, the city gardens, new public library, built of white stone, patterned in the Greek style, after the Library of Athens, the Harvard Preparatory Medical School, Academy of Arts and Sciences, Old South Church, moved and changed. I enjoyed this sight-seeing thoroughly. The Notre Dame Sisters were very familiar. Sr. Bernardine, the reverend mother of the convent, is a lovely lady, of superior character and excellent address. She made many inquiries respecting our San Jose college, and evinced a gratifying interest in California. "To a wayfarer in a strange land nothing is so sweet as to hear his name on the tongue of a friend," remarks the sage Egyptian in " Ben Hur," and I may add that it is equally as cheering to hear the dear names of our loved ones mentioned by strangers, as I experienced when Sister Bernardine asked if I knew Sister Anna Raphael, my beloved cousin and former teacher, and her sister, Miss Marcella Fitzgerald, than whom I have not a more valued friend in California, and so I felt the sweet thrill in my heart as happily as though the names were my own. Returning to the hotel about eleven o'clock, finding the other members prepared, Dr. F. offered to conduct our party of five across the Charles River, over the bridge immortalized by America's poet laureate, to "Cambridge, the classic," and I do not recall having ever enjoyed a day more replete with pleasure.

Our guide, a graduate of Harvard, and later of a Vienna medical college, left no effort untried to render the occasion enjoyable, and his exertions were indeed appreciated by my friends and self with truly Californian enthusiasm. He presented his fellow student and friend, Dr. Barnes, a worthy practitioner of Cambridge, who at once joined us, and accompanied us to the home of Longfellow, which we inspected with almost reverence. The mansion is now in possession of the poet's daughter, who at present is away from home, and the hospitable housekeeper extended the honors. The doctor led the way to the study of the author of "Hiawatha," and showed all the articles of interest therein.

Taking advantage of the privilege I sat in the prettily-carved heavy chestnutwood easy chair, made from the tree under which stood the "Village Blacksmith's" shop, and presented to the poet by the children of Cambridge, mentioned in the poem, together with a small watercolor picture of tree and shop. I was given his pen to handle, and, with indescribable emotion, and wishing for a single thought worthy of the master mind that had swayed this weapon "mightier than the sword," I tremblingly wrote a line suggestive of the occasion in my autograph book. The writing desk and table remain as Mr. Longfellow left it, and are likely to be guarded from the curious as long as the vigilant housekeeper continues in charge. A painting of the poet, by his son Ernest, stands on an easel near the table. The work is inferior, and the portrait poor. Books lie around in artistic disorder, and the room is as pretty as it is interesting. Across the hall we were shown into the Washington room, where our first president made his headquarter's comfortable, as general of the American Army.

In the absence of the family we deemed further inspection intrusive, and took our departure, filled with a happy memory. As we passed out, we noticed the Charles River gleaming beyond, and remembered that it was a favorite theme of the poet's, and his verses welled up into expression, which we quoted, closing the gate, and threw back a kiss to the dear old home of our favorite. Following up the avenue we came to Elmwood, the Lowell homestead, where most of the poet's papers were written. Strange, I had a letter of introduction to James Russell Lowell, but he sickened and died the week before I arrived.

Retracing our path, Drs F. and B. took us to Harvard University, all through which we were shown, the different buildings, and the museum, a most complete and beautifully appointed institution. California is here prominently represented by an enormous octopus, extending across the ceiling of an extensive exhibition room. The gymnasium, refectory, and theater, memorial hall, and other excellent departments, were most interesting. Next we were conveyed to the old elm, under whose shade Washington received command of the army, July 3, 1775, and which still throws its cloak of green over those standing anear, who read the lines upon the granite that prove how much respect to it is due. Vandalism is obviated by plates of tin fastened over the scars made by iconoclastic hands. A shower of leaves fell around me as I paused beside the iron railing encircling the venerated tree, and I caught some of them as souvenirs of the honored place. As it has continually showered throughout our peregrinations in Cambridge, I find the "rainy day" of Longfellow most lifelike, for—

"With each gust the dead leaves fall,
And the day is dark and cold and dreary."

The vines are clinging everywhere, and how smooth and regular is their clustering wilderness of beauty. We contemplate a stroll or drive through Mt. Auburn Cemetery, the Westminster of America, but the rain, the incessant rain, drives us back, so we reluctantly return to Boston, leaving for another day Auburn's storied dead. Now our program calls for a thorough inspection of Boston, and how I will enjoy this sight-seeing in the old historic city! I like it best of anything I have seen outside of California, the dear old State, which, "taken all in all, we ne'er shall see" her "like again."

Entering the stately Vendome in a most forlorn and bedraggled condition, we hasten to our apartments to make preparations for dinner, which we expect to enjoy, the "inner man" having been neglected during our loiter in Cambridge. After dinner my friend returned to Worcester.

Saturday, August 29.

This morning's sunny hours were spent down town shopping, among the queerly crooked streets. The day has been charmingly bright, and everything conducive to enjoyment of the outing. We bought souvenirs and other nicknacks—perhaps I ought to designate them as "Yankee notions."

Noontide found us lunching, and later, accompanied by Dr. F., we inspected the Museum of Arts and Sciences, where two hours were instructively spent. How I wish I could remember all I saw in this treasure-filled museum of art!

Thence our escort guided us to the North or Christ Church, from whose tall "belfry arch" gleamed the lanterns of Paul Revere in 1775, a beacon warning to the people of Charlestown of the march of the British soldiery from town, "down to their boats on the shore." If memory were lax in retaining the impressions of history, the immortal measure of Longfellow, familiar to every schoolchild, would supply the mental vision with a poetic picture of this ride.

"Through all our history, to the last,
In the hour of darkness, and peril, and need,
The people will waken and listen to hear
The hurrying hoof beats of that steed,
And the midnight message of Paul Revere."

Mrs. Murphy presented me with "The Midnight Ride" souvenir orange spoon, a beautifully etched representation of the hero wildly riding to "spread the alarm."

Near by is "Old Copp's Hill Burial Ground," and thither we wended our meanderings, and had no occasion to regret an introduction to Mr. Edward McDonald, the intelligent superintendent, who has diligently searched the archives for history of the place and every tomb in the cemetery, and has compiled the result of his labor in neat book form.

On Copp's Hill, where we stand, "Generals Burgoyne and Clinton watched the battle on Bunker Hill, and directed the battery." Within shadow of the hill stands Boston's oldest homestead, and Christ Church, erected in 1723, is said to be the oldest but one public building in Boston. "The prayer books and communion silver, given by George II., in 1733, are now in use." The church also contains a bust of Washington, which was the first ever made of the "Father of his country." The chime of bells, conveyed from England, is the most ancient chime in America, dated 1744.

One of the oldest gravestones in this cemetery is dated 1661, and I remarked that the slabs are of slate, the first I have seen. The inscriptions are cut into the stone, in primitive lettering. The tombstone said to be the oldest in New England, according to Mr. McDonald's pamphlet, is here, erected to the memory of Grace Berry, who died in Plymouth, in 1625. When Copp's Hill was opened first as a burial ground, her remains were interred herein, in the year 1659. Among the most interesting inscriptions I read, the one over the grave of Cotton Mather attracted my particular attention, and I freely transcribe the wording to my notebook:—

"The Reverend Doctors,
   Increase, Cotton,
   & Samuel Mather
   were interred in this vault.
'Tis the tomb of our Father's
   Mather——Crocker's
   I. Died Augt. 27th, 1723, æ 84.
   C. Died Feb. 13th, 1727, æ 65.
   S. Died June 27th, 1785, æ 79."

We were shown where stood a large willow tree, planted in the Ellis plot in 1844, which was a cutting from the tree over Napoleon's grave at St. Helena. The grave of Amos Lincoln was pointed out, with the information that he was one of the many young colonists who overthrew the cargo of tea in Boston Harbor, and afterwards married a daughter of Paul Revere.

I copied the following epitaph, which for peculiarity struck my fancy:—

"In memory of
   Mary Huntley
Who departed this life Sep. 28th, 1798,
   in the 64th year of her age.
   "Stop here, my friend, and cast an eye.
      As you are now, so once was I;
      As I am now, so you must be.
      Prepare for death and follow me."

A wag, upon perusing the warning, added:—
   "To follow you I'm not content,
      Unless I know which way you went."

From the historic spot, filled with the "silent majority" of Puritan heroes, we were guided to Faneuil Hall, with its big "gold" grasshopper vane. The dear old building has been devoted to the uses of a market, but, were speech possible, what stories it could tell—hot-headed debate and earnest appeal, warm applause and final triumph. The edifice (for is it not dedicated to our country, which claims us, after God?) remains about as when the colonists met herein and read the immortal Declaration which proclaimed them free and independent people. Everything suggestive of the Revolutionary days is held in almost sacred respect in Boston, and Faneuil Hall building, used as a market place, is not, indeed, in depreciation of its historic character, but to check the corroding influence of idleness, time's wearying enemy.

Strolling onward we reached Granary Cemetery, wherein are interred the remains of John Hancock, the fearless signer, with other witnesses of the Declaration, Benjamin Franklin and Paul Revere. Every name inscribed on the bronze gate "cometh up as a flower" from the ground of early learned history lessons, and pondering over the dust these sacred precincts inclose is a source of novel interest to me, time having exorcised the dormitory of endless sleep of the spirit of melancholy.

The little short street, or court, where Daniel Webster and Rufus Choate were wont to walk together for hours and discuss the important affairs of State, was attractive indeed, and I was shown the hotel wherein the two statesmen dropped ever and anon to moisten their throats, seared by dry subjects. This hotel, by the way, was rendered famous by the facetious remark of Artemus Ward in loquaciously locating Harvard University on its third floor (and the lawn facing the Conservatory of Music), it being a resort for the "students on a lark."

Wending homeward, or, rather, hotelward, we bent our course to the Charles River, took a long look at the dark waters, rippling and shimmering in the different electric and gas lights in lengthened brilliancy.

Reaching the Vendome, we dined, and did justice to the repast, after which my companions attended the theater, the doctor spent his evening with a medical friend, and I repaired to my room to write home and prepare for rest.

Sunday, August 30.

We arose early to take a trip planned by Dr. F. to Gloucester and Salem, to meet Dr. Oliver Wendell Holmes, and my heart bounded with delight in anticipation of the great pleasure in store for us, but

"Pleasures are as poppies spread;
Pull the flower and the bloom is shed."

The merciless rain persistently imprisoned us within doors, and my hopes vanished like "chaff before the wind."

We attended mass at the cathedral and Church of the Immaculate Conception, then visited Boston College. We were shown all through the institution, and then drove home, not, however, without being allowed the wonderful privilege of a peep at John L. Sullivan's saloon.

Well, we wrote letters all day, entertained each other as well as the dark day allowed, and during the afternoon I went out walking with a friend, who conducted me to Boston Harbor, whereat arose visions of the active "tea party." Vessels bound for New York and other places were quietly lying at the wharf, and the city was peculiarly noiseless. This is my first experience of a Puritan Sabbath. Even the tinkling bells on the horses of street cars were removed, lest they sound too gay and loud for the standard solemnity of Sunday.

The rain abating we wandered along Beacon Street Hill, where my companion called my attention to the colonial style of building, and the ancient green glass window panes. Through Dr. Holmes' "Long Walk" of the

Commons we returned to the hotel. Throwing off my wraps I found my feet damp, the only uncomfortable result of my jaunt. After dinner our self-kindly-appointed escort returned to his home, and we late birds retired at two o'clock A. M.

Monday, August 31.

We remained within doors to-day, having nothing particular to do, yet we cannot leave here until to-morrow night, as accommodations on the steamer *Plymouth, via* "the Sound," can only be afforded us then. We were exceedingly late for breakfast, having arisen at nearly noontide, so were served in the small dining hall without regard to the menu. This afternoon I visited friends in Worcester, and was shown the beauties of that city,—the park Lake Quinsigamund, the summer resort of the Chautauquan Association, and upon whose waters the Harvard boys practice the graceful, manly art of rowing, when preparing for a contest, also the home and birthplace of Bancroft, the great historian, and other points of interest. We returned on the evening train, and all retired about midnight, my cousins having been to the theater.

September 1.

During the fresh, rosy hours of the morning

we remained at home and wrote our letters. During the afternoon we went for a walk through the crooked, magnetic thoroughfares, and Mrs. Murphy bought a lot of Boston tea to take home with her, to dispense to her guests of the sewing circle, when recounting her peregrinations through the esthetic city of learning. We made some purchases, souvenirs of New England, and over the soft, green carpet of the storied Commons returned to our temporary quarters, noting on our way the glistening frog pond and historic elm that witnessed the persecution of witches, and other uncanny ceremonies of the very early Puritan days, all speaking of an anxious past linked strongly to the peace-crowned present.

We visited the church of Rev. Phillips Brooks, which, I am told, has the finest and one of the best-appointed church organs in America, the second finest being in the Tabernacle at Salt Lake City.

Towards evening our trunks were packed for New York, and we prepared for traveling. We left the beautiful "Vendome" for the Old Colony Railroad Office, and took the Fall River line for Gotham. We entered the palace car "Lilac" at seven o'clock, and soon were whirling away from Boston. I left the beautiful city I have learned to love, for its classic associations and historcial interest. with regret, as some of the most instructive moments of my life have just been experienced here Viewing the quiet, homelike mansions of the great and grand Cambridge, where stalwart minds have worked and rested, was a pleasure to be enjoyed by me but once in life, and I earnestly wish I could repeat it.

We arrived at Fall River at 8:30, and boarded the *Plymouth*, a perfect little floating palace, exquisitely ornamented interiorly, and illuminated by myriads of electric jets. The furniture throughout is handsome. "The Lowell String Band," of ten pieces, discourses music for the delectation of the passengers. We are an hour late in starting, it being now ten o'clock, whereas we should have been steaming up the river at nine. The call, "All ashore who are going ashore," must be a signal that we soon shall start. The music continues; at times the strains are most excruciating. How keen must have been the torture of the witches, if these musicians are the descendants of the old colonists!

At 10:20 we start. We retire at eleven. Our staterooms are neat, convenient, and comfortable.

CHAPTER VI.

GLIMPSES OF NEW YORK CITY.

Wednesday, September 2.

WE appear in sight of New York City early and come out to take a look at Long Island Sound, and, later, our destination, under low-hanging masses of fog. The first building "greeting our coming" is an immense insane asylum, and on our left, farther on is Blackwell's Island, with its gray stone prisons and glistening cannon. As we approach I observe hundreds of women of the Island Reformatory, wearing large straw hats, in ranks, walking around enjoying the morning air and sunshine. We pass under Brooklyn Bridge at nine o'clock, having sped past the *Puritan* coming up the Sound, although she left Boston two hours ahead of us.

We were conducted to a carriage by the porter, and were soon "in line" trying to make way to the Fifth Avenue Hotel. The streets were dense with vehicles of every known description, rendering progress difficult. However, at last we registered at the Fifth Avenue, and upon reaching our rooms our California mail was sent to us, and with indescribable avidity I devoured the contents of four letters from home, the first missives I have had from the loved ones, with whom it seems an age since I parted. I answered all, and wrote a note to a friend in Baltimore, informing him of our arrival in New York, and likelihood of reaching "Maryland, my Maryland" within a few weeks. We then waited for our trunks, that never came —until evening.

Mrs. B. D. Murphy went out for a walk, to look for her old home, and familiar objects in its vicinity. With Martin she drove to the Bank of Donahue, Kelly & Co., to present her letters of credit. In her absence Mr. Malone called, and kindly offered to be of use, knowing our inexperience in traveling, and possible inconvenience we might encounter in a strange city.

We dined in our parlor and the rest of the party attended the Lyceum Theater, returning about midnight, when we retired. I had devoted the hours of their absence to reading, and endeavoring to decipher the stenography of this crude diary.

September 3.

With the first smile of dawn came up Mr.

Shriver's card. As I had arisen, and was ready for breakfast, I went down to meet him. He had received my note of the day previous, and, traveling at night, had reached New York City about six this morning. He gave us a cordial welcome to the East, which warm greeting was succeeded by a friendly offer of himself as escort for the day. After chatting awhile we were joined by my cousins, and all breakfasted, and went immediately to do some shopping, Mr. S. acting as guide. Gorham's elegant display of silverware was supervised, and from the rich assortment of unique designs Mrs. M. selected several dozen exquisitely wrought souvenir spoons, together with rare bits of art, things "of beauty," that cannot fail to be " a joy forever" to those fortunate enough to possess them through the little lady's generosity of heart and purse.

We thoroughly enjoyed Tiffany's Art Rooms, and wished we could spend a week among the bric-a-brac alone. Next dry goods houses were visited, and wherever shopping was to be done, until, tired and weary, we returned to lunch. Then Mr. S. took Mrs. M. and myself on the elevated railroad to Benziger Bros., away down town. I bought some souvenirs for friends, and Mrs. Murphy made her usual liberal purchases. Mr. S. showed me the "little church 'round the corner," which edifice I was anxious to look at, and many other places of interest claimed my attention when pointed out by one so intelligently capable of instructing the uninformed. I came back pleased with our outing. Mr. S. invited us to attend the fireworks on Weehawken Heights, Hoboken, New Jersey, but Martin had tickets for the theater.

We dined at 7:30, and Mrs. Murphy spent the evening with her uncle, Mr. Green, Mr. S. accompanying her thither, the trio, Martin, Maud, and Evie, attending the theater. I read, and wrote my letters, until the return of my friends.

I do not like the climate of New York at this season; it is unpleasant, the air being moist, and the heat oppressive.

September 4.

"Up with the lark," and prepared for the day, arranged my trunk, and chased time until eleven o'clock, when the rest of the party were ready. Mr. Eugene Kelly called on Mrs. Murphy, and took Martin down town. After breakfast Mr. Shriver appeared in time to accompany us to Lord & Taylor's, the suit house. Procuring a conveyance suitable for the occasion, he drove us through Central Park, a ride I was most desirous of taking, to see the oft-heard-of public breathing-place of America's greatest city. I always speak for myself and may say here that I am delighted with what I see about me in this beautiful sylvan retreat, with the pleasant outing and the agreeable company.

Upon our return our escort guided us on the elevated railroad to the Battery, and up the Produce Exchange Building to the tower, two hundred and forty feet high, fourteen stories, whence we obtained an excellent view of the city—Castle Garden almost under us, Governor's Island just beyond, where General Hancock was stationed some years before his death, Bedloe's Island, with the "Liberty" statue, Brooklyn Bridge, East River, the Hudson, Staten Island, the Narrows, or Gate, Perth-Amboy beyond Staten Island, all delineated so perfectly and charmingly as to be a picture in the gallery of memory forever. Although enchanted with the scene and occasion, after an hour's contemplation of the busy city under us, we descended and were shown Wall Street, where fabulous fortunes have been made and lost within a day. It is a narrow highway, of a few blocks, stretching towards East River, and but for its name would never arrest attention. We stood at the entrance of Trinity Church, almost classic in its ancient dignity, then sauntered leisurely to the building containing the offices of Jay Gould,

Russell Sage, and other notable personages of the metropolis; and, indeed, many other sights claimed us, which my weary head cannot recall.

Taking the cars, we returned to the hotel very tired. Shortly thereafter Mr. S. introduced his sister, Mrs. T. J. Myer, and her two daughters, of Maryland, to our party, who are *en route* for home, from a visit to Boston, Dedham, and, later, Newport. Mrs. Myer is a rather tall, stout lady, with comely features, kindly expression, and dignified mien. Gently welcoming our "California delegation" East, she warmly and hospitably invited us to visit her home in Maryland, all of which I appreciate, being a stranger in a strange place.

After dinner Mr. Shriver took us all to Weehawken Heights, on the Jersey side of the Hudson, the vicinity being the scene, if I mistake not, of the Hamilton-Burr duel—now called Hoboken. The little five-minute trip across the river is peculiarly pleasing, the many gas, electric, and other lights illuminating the rippling waters, and the colored lights of the vessels giving life and beauty to the strange, sparkling scene.

We were conveyed to the amphitheater, and there witnessed the El Dorado extravaganza of King Solomon, which was elegantly presented, with seven hundred persons participating at once. The rich dresses, graceful posing, and agreeable singing were most enchanting, and altogether the play was entirely distinct from anything I have ever witnessed. The arena was arranged in the open air, on the Heights, the sky forming the canopy, and when the walls of Jerusalem were burned, the smoke ascended, circulated in the air, and disappeared into space as naturally and gracefully as possible.

We next attended the fireworks, then sat and listened to the concert, at which Mr. Levy, the cornetist, was to have played, but he failing to appear we returned to the ferry, and home. There were eleven in the party, and we enjoyed the unique evening's entertainment very much, with the cool dews of night glistening over our raiment in the radiance of a thousand lights.

Saturday, September 5.

We were up and about at eight o'clock. After breakfast our escort conducted us to the Hoffman House, to see the works of art displayed in the salon—"Satyr, and the Nymphs" of Bougereau, a "St. John in the Wilderness"(?) by Correggio, a fine piece of work representing Port Marseilles, valued at $25,000, some chaste statuary, and other articles of vertu. He then suggested a look at the

Eden Musée, where are to be seen the waxworks after the house of Madame Tussaud in London, the royal heads of Europe, a bevy of Confederate and Federal soldiers of the late war, prominent musicians, actors, and actresses, great men of the day, etc. Below we enter the "Chamber of Horrors." Here most heart-thrilling scenes are depicted to the life. Why is Millet's "*Angelus*" presented in wax in the Chamber of *Horrors?* "The Guillotine," "Eyraud," the brutal murderer of Gouffe, "Judith and Holofernes," "Charlotte Corday," "The Lion's Bride," "Execution by Electricity," are all appropriately in place representing horror, but *why* "The Angelus"?

A funny incident happened as we were passing from one hall to the next. The word "paint" in large letters was attached to the back of a bench, and a gentleman had just arisen from the seat and was seriously contemplating the damage wrought on his new stylish trousers by the contact. The expression of regret was so apparent on his countenance that we pitied his misfortune, until Evie exclaimed: "The goose! Couldn't he see 'paint' big enough to warn him, if he didn't smell it?" "A light breaks in upon our brain"—the immobility of the figure suggested that it was wax. We felt foolish, but enjoyed the amusing occurrence to its fullest.

The art gallery of the Musée is full of treasures, and well worth a visit, but time is flying, and we must leave these truly realistic scenes for our own active ones of life.

I accompanied Mrs. Murphy on another shopping tour, and when we returned to the hotel, at six o'clock P. M., we were very tired, faint, and hungry. I feel the depressing effects of the climate, possibly the result on a constitution unused to close, moist, oppressive heat. The Baltimore party left for home on the three o'clock train, having called to say *adios* during our absence. The trio went to the theater in the evening. Mrs. M. arranged her purchases, packed them into trunks for home going, and about eleven o'clock we gladly welcomed "nature's sweet restorer." Was somewhat homesick this afternoon and telegraphed to my sisters at the dear old home, the like of which I have not yet seen.

Sunday, September 6.

I was prepared and ready for church at 8:30; the rest of the company appeared at nine, when we breakfasted and attended the Jesuits' Church of St. Francis Xavier at half past eleven. We called at the Academy of the Sacred Heart, where Mrs. Murphy had studied in her girlhood, and felt inclined to review the earlier scenes supplied by faithful memory. Introducing ourselves as *Californians*, always a talismanic title in the East, we were gently invited within, and entertained by a sweet-faced, angelic-mannered lady in the garb of the order. After many inquiries about our happy land, she softly asked if any of us knew of Kern County, in California. I responded in the affirmative, whereupon she questioned me about a nephew from whom she had not heard for a year or more, and about him she was very anxious. Mentioning his name, I was surprised to learn that the young man was one who had brought me letters of introduction from Virginia, and had visited my home just two weeks prior to my departure on this trip. It was with strange pleasure that I afforded the good lady the information she sought. The coincidence was a peculiar one. Madame O'R. was clever and kind, but with this new friend we soon had to part, to return to lunch.

Although it was raining, and close, yet we took a carriage drive to Brooklyn, over the famous bridge. We counted forty churches in sight and about concluded that "of a verity" Brooklyn is the "city of churches."

While driving all through Greenwood Cemetery, the day merged into a beautiful afternoon, with occasional showers. Here the rich and the great are interred. It appeared a vast park, with beautiful driveways, ponds, trees, shrubbery, lawns, and endless varieties of flowers. James Gordon Bennett's plot is remarkable for an elegant piece of pure white Italian marble, sculptured by a master hand, representing a woman in the attitude of prayer, whose vesture's folds stand out in broad relief as though fluttered by a passing zephyr. The tomb of the Stewarts and other men of wealth are to be seen without introduction. We were shown the grave and monument of Charlotte Canda, aged seventeen, who was thrown from her carriage and killed when going to attend a party given in honor of her birthday. The monument is a beautifully chiseled marble in form of a shrine inclosing the figure of a sweet virginal girl, suggestive of our "Lady of Lourdes," so prettily carved and chaste looking in its graceful robes folded softly around her standing form. Many, many elegant mausoleums called attention by the superiority of their artistic worth, but could not be mentioned in a hasty notebook like this.

Recrossing the bridge, which alone is a new sensation to us, we reached the Fifth Avenue Hotel, and dined at seven, after having spent a delightful afternoon.

Mrs. Murphy and Martin went out early in

the evening for her "Uncle Green." The enervating effects of the sultry climate have prostrated Evie; she could not accompany us to Brooklyn, and has been ill nearly all day. Mr. Green returned with Mrs. M. and spent the evening with us. He is a very nice old gentleman, and an interesting, well-informed talker. Possessing an artist soul he is by profession a sculptor, and I enjoyed conversing with him.

September 7.

This morning I received letters from home. How happy it makes me to hear from there! Later we repeated a shopping tour, then returned to luncheon, expecting Mr. Kelly, who invited Mrs. M. for a drive through the park. This being Labor day, many of the stores were closed, a miserable demonstration and procession showing slightly how the occasion is honored. The day is bright, but again sultry. Mr. Kelly did not appear.

September 8.

I was up with the dawn, and partook of our matin meal at eleven. Spent the morning in the stores with Mrs. Murphy, and the afternoon down town with Maud and Evalyn, a new experience for us. I am getting tired of New York, and would like a lungful of good, light, fresh air. I feel very weak after my jaunt around town. The god of sleep offers particularly acceptable charms, and I resign myself to blissful slumber, while the rest attend the theater.

CHAPTER VII.

A TRIP UP THE HUDSON.

September 9.

ADMISSION day of California! This morning we took the steamer *Albany* for a trip up the Hudson, to Albany, and were nine hours on the water. The views on both sides are as picturesque as some I have seen of the Rhine; the water is as smooth as glass at times, and again in undulating waves sweeps nobly to the sea. I am told the river varies from a mile to two miles in width, and in the bays it is from three to four miles in breadth. It originally had several names, the French calling it "Rio de Montaigne;" the Dutch designated this vast arm of the sea "Mauritius," after the Nassaun Prince Maurice. The Indian names are numerous and appropriate. "The Hudson" was finally settled as the proper title by the English in honor of Henry Hudson, who was an Englishman, although under Dutch auspices. He first explored the river from the now metropolis to the capital in 1609.

Taking our chairs on the deck of the well-appointed steamer, comfortably wrapped, a brisk breeze fanning our faces, God's perfect sunshine smiling on us, the panorama of grandeur unfolds before us. On the right, or east bank, the Manhattanville College of the Christian Brothers, and elegant adjoining convent, loom up amid the trees, reposeful in their clustering wood, which "crescents more than half the lawn." Soon follows the home of Audubon, the ornithologist. On the west bank the Palisades, in their columnar strength, buffet wind and wave for fifteen miles. They are of "basaltic trap-rock" formation. Next I note the home of James Gordon Bennett, on Washington Heights, where Fort Washington stood when taken by the English in 1776. Fort Lee stands on the western bank. Stewart Castle, on the summit of the Heights, is grand and lordly in its position of superiority and elegance. The Palisades continue on the west side, and the end of Manhattan Island is reached as we approach Spuyten Duyval Creek and station.

The landscape, including Riverdale, is a series of pretty scenes, perfect poems of nature. Fort Hill Castle, the former property of Edwin Forest, the tragedian, was purchased for the Convent of Mount St. Vincent, which stately building stands in prominent view near the river's edge, sloping lawns and tree-girt paths forming a tasteful foreground.

Yonkers is next in sight, with its notable feature, the old Phillipse Manor, conspicuous midst the leafy wold. It was built in 1682, and used occasionally by General Washington during the early struggle for independence.

Passing Glenwood (this is the third place of the name I have seen since leaving California we are regaled with a lovely view of "Greystone," the handsome home of the late Hon. Samuel J. Tilden. Within cool shades of kindly green, uprearing its gray front to the sun, the mansion, characteristic of its late owner's life, is open to inspection, and like him, too, in that it is without flaw.

The Palisades rise higher, reaching as they stretch onward over five hundred feet, until the boundary line between New York and New Jersey is gained, when they abruptly cease. Dobb's Ferry is pointed out to me as the place where the intercessors for Major Andre's life met General Greene, "president of the court which condemned him to death."

"Sunnyside," the charming cottage of our gentle Irving, embowered in foliage and made up of gable ends," is the most interesting villa in Irvington, "the classic and poetic spot of our country."

The residence of Jay Gould, on the old Paulding property, is a castle-like structure, imposingly handsome, yet my interest is more keenly pointed to Tarrytown, where rest the remains of Washington Irving, in Sleepy Hollow Churchyard. A simple stone, modestly inscribed, "Washington Irving, born April 3, 1783, died Nov. 28, 1859," shows the place of his burial.

Here, too, near the village Andre was captured, and on the spot has been erected a monument commemorative of the event. Strange to note that, coincident with the traitor Arnold's death in England, the tree under which Andre was caught was killed by lightning in the second year of this century.

The village of Nyack is on our left, or on the west bank, nestling among the hills. Sing-Sing Prison buildings are made of marble, and the town is quite a large, pretty settlement, with pleasant homes and fine residences.

The next place of interest is the Croton Works; they supply the metropolis with water, an extensive aqueduct conveying sixty million gallons a day to the Central Park reservoir.

A flash of history rushes to memory at sight of Stony Point, whose fort was recaptured by mad Anthony Wayne in Revolutionary days. The banks of the Hudson teem with historic lore, yet I may only note places familiar to my unsophisticated mind through reading, and memory of American history, which is fast fading for lack of review.

The ruins of Fort Independence are at Peekskill, which also embraces the birthplace and death scene of John Paulding, one of Andre's captors. Near the village is the country seat of the late Henry Ward Beecher.

Next on the west bank is Captain Kidd's Point. We all know the story of that adventurous mariner and his pirate crew. The crags known as Dunderbergh, described by Irving, are sublimely picturesque, but lacking the "tumbling imps" and malignant spirits who visited dangerous squalls upon the Dutch sea captains that failed in respect to the goblin ruler.

West Point commands attention on the bluff overlooking the pacific waters of the Hudson, on our left, and is grandly situated. During the Revolution General Arnold the afterward unhappy traitor, was in command of this stronghold. "History tells the rest."

Continuing our "voyage" and admiring the restful look of the beautiful scenery, enraptured with the views, at times reaching sublimity, we come to Newbergh, where the noble old Father of His Country refused the honors of kingship, and afterwards disbanded his army.

At noon we descended to the dining saloon and took lunch. The meal was not what we expected, and was hardly enjoyable, so we again contented ourselves on deck, the cabin being close and "stuffy."

Poughkeepsie, beautifully located, is called the "Queen City of the Hudson." It is full of fine residences, and has a large population, who appreciate the patriotic interest which the city enjoys, having held the State Legislature when New York was in possession of the British, in 1777. We pass under Poughkeepsie Bridge, a valuable enterprise which connects the East with the mines of Pennsylvania.

Watching forward, without notes for some distance, I rest my thoughts, but I take up the strain as we near the Caatskills—the dreamland of poor old Rip Van Winkle, the master character of Irving, which will live as long as the Hudson flows. It is not for my feeble pen to attempt a picture of the mountains, it takes an Irving to delineate in golden wording. I am satisfied to gaze upon the woody uplands that kept the admiring attention of our charming writer and historian of the Hudson, until they "melt into hazy distance," and, gazing in enchanted reverie, my heart goes out to poet, artist, sculptor, and actor, for each is keeping vivid the fairy charms depicted of these highlands by the chaste and gentle Irving.

The air is so fresh and bracing that one cannot remain long under the dreamy influence. There is a station on the east bank called Stuyvesant, after the old Dutch governor, and somewhere hereabouts resided Martin Van Buren. The Convent of the Sacred Heart stands high on the western slope, and is an elegant institution, conducted by the "Madames" for the higher education of young ladies. The old manor house of the Van Rensselaers still rests on the eastern shore, and is certainly a "relic of antiquity," for it was built in 1640.

Resting my eyes I await the arrival of our steamboat at the capital, which we reach at six o'clock—one hundred and forty-four miles from New York City, and I'm glad to land.

A sensational experience awaited us upon leaving the boat. The hotel men were screaming the names of the houses they represented and pulling passengers every way but the one they wished to go. They kept up the deafening sounds, confusing and unpleasant, until we were safely within a coach. We aimed for the "Delavan," where we registered.

After supper we took a carriage for a drive around the city. We were shown the magnificent Statehouse, which they tell me has cost seventeen millions already, and when completed will exceed in size the capitol at Washington.

It is certainly a noble structure, but as yet unfinished.

We enjoyed the Washington Driving Park, in which stands a bronze statue of Robert Burns, erected by the Scotch citizens. An artificial lake underlies fine sheltering trees, a shining gem of beauty. Thence the homes of lumbermen, bankers, merchants, and business men attracted our attention, as they face the park on Inglewood Place, and are perfect dreams of luxury. I was desirous of seeing some of the old Dutch houses, and saw one of the oldest in Albany. It stands on a corner, a quaint old brick building used as a grocery store, and is marked in large figures 1710.

The city is large, wealthy, and influential, and, being New York's capital, how could it be otherwise?

Having seen all we could, Mrs. Murphy remained with me in the hotel, while Martin took Maud and Evie to the theater. They returned about eleven o'clock, and we prepared to retrace our trip to New York City *via* New York and Hudson River Railroad, leaving Albany at 1:30, arriving in New York City at six o'clock this morning. It was a pleasant, bright trip. I enjoyed the few hours' rest afforded by the cars coming down the east bank of the storied Hudson.

CHAPTER VIII.

THE CITY OF BROTHERLY LOVE.

Thursday, September 10.

IMMEDIATELY upon arriving we retired to our rooms for a rest. We found letters from home and Baltimore. During the day we visited St. Patrick's Cathedral, on Fifth Avenue, a large, grand edifice of white stone, with handsomely carved marble altars. I did not particularly admire the elegant structure, as it appeared to me cold interiorly, and exteriorly seemed to suggest itself a monument to the architect's skill, without the inviting air which calls, "Ye that are weary and heavy laden," etc. The steps leading to the door of the superb edifice are few, which is an advantage, and the symmetrical harmony of the building is not marred by the peculiar idea of economy which places a hall beneath, to the inconvenience of churchgoers, especially old people whose climbing days are over.

I went down town with Mrs. Murphy and to call on Fr. Healey, West Fourteenth Street, but found him not. Returning to the hotel, we dined late, and Martin took Maud and Evie to the theater.

Fr. Healey came to spend the evening. He was a playmate of Mrs. M.'s New York childhood, and was pleased to see her. He is a bright, intelligent man, whom I am happy to meet. He kindly invited us to Coney Island to spend a day with his sister and other relatives, but our arrangements to leave here are almost completed. He contemplates attending the funeral to-morrow of Mrs. Riordan, mother of the late Rev. J. J. Riordan, founder of the Emigrants' Home, Castle Garden.

September 11.

Arose at 8:30 and prepared my baggage for Baltimore *via* Philadelphia. After breakfast we took the ferryboat about eleven o'clock, crossed the North or Hudson River into New Jersey, and boarded the Pennsylvania train *en route* for the Quaker City.

We soon cross the river over the drawbridge, and stop at Newark, a fine, thriving city, whose birth antedates the Revolution. Then, skimming onward, we pass a station marked "Waverley." The country looks well for farming and grazing; the trees are extensively spread but small sized. Elizabeth is the name of another station and town. We are rapidly passing many others, but I find it difficult to catch the lettering, the train is speeding so swiftly.

Menlo Park is a familiar title, where stands a pretty village with pleasure grounds and drives, natural trees and shrubbery, shady and fresh looking. Gazing about and longing for information, enjoying all I can see, I drop my pencil until coming into Morrisville, Pennsylvania, after which I note Landreth's Farm and Garden Seed Place, founded in 1780. It is a prosperous appearing, extensive estate. The broad lands of Pennsylvania are excellent for ranching purposes, and there are many richly laden orchards scattered around in sight.

Germantown Junction is called, and, looking out, I behold smoking chimneys everywhere, and suppose we have entered a manufacturing city of no mean importance. I wonder if my memory is correct in locating this as the place occupied by the British when surprised by Washington in 1777.

Leaving the smokestacks of Germantown we cross the river and gain the city of Philadelphia, where thought is lost in the sea of immense buildings and uniform rows of brick dwellings.

We took a room at the Lafayette Hotel for the day, and partook of a midday dinner, then ordered a carriage and drove around the city, through Fairmount Park, for four hours. The charming drive along the banks of the beautiful Schuylkill was indeed enjoyable, and I took special pleasure in noting the perfect views of varied scenery.

We rode over the Centennial Fair Grounds, and noted Memorial Hall, 1876, as the monument of that great year, remaining in the park, also the superb fountain erected by the Maryland citizens of Philadelphia, being a gigantic figure of Moses as a centerpiece, standing upon a firm foundation of massive rock. Around this imposing form are the handsome marble full-size statues of Father Matthew, the Apostle of Temperance, Charles Carroll, of Carrollton, the fearless Signer, Most Rev. John Carroll, the first Archbishop of Baltimore, and Commodore John Barry, the illustrious Wexford man, who so ably distinguished himself in the American naval service. Here, also, is a basaltic column from the Giant's Causeway, Ireland, duly inscribed. A large figure of Christopher Columbus also adorns a place in the park, presented by the Italian citizens. A fine statue in bronze on a granite pedestal of General Meade is an attractive feature.

The house of William Penn was shown us, which we viewed with curiosity and interest.

It is certainly a relic, and well prized by the State bearing the good old Quaker's name. A statue of Jeanne D'Arc and a beautiful marble of Niobe are exquisite pieces of art.

Boating on the river is a most pleasurable pastime, and I think much time could be happily spent amid these scenes of sylvan beauty. The superb Statehouse, supplanting the historic one which held the cracked bell of liberty for so many years, Wanamaker's stores, and a thousand other objects of note, were seen and talked over by our vigilant little band.

At 7:30 P. M. we took the Pennsylvania line for Baltimore, dining on the car, with mirth and jollity for salt and spice. At 9:45 we were ushered into the city of noble Calvert, and were considerably amused when searching for conveyances to the Rennert House. Nothing better than old rattletrap hacks were presented, and finally our party was divided up for occupancy of two coupés and "rattled o'er the stony street," at a "two-forty rate," to our destination. The city seemed perfectly still.

Registering at the Rennert, we were assigned to rather pleasant rooms, and retired to rest at midnight. The ominous mosquito bar enveloping the couches took me back in spirit to Stockton, California, where Julia Weber one night kept guard over my slumbers lest the "galley nippers" from the sloughs invade the meshes of the netting and leave me "without eyes," as she quaintly expressed it.

CHAPTER IX.

A VISIT WITH CARDINAL GIBBONS.

Saturday, September 12.

EARLY bird and luckless worm, which is which in this instance? I am up and prepared for breakfast, when a friend's card appears, so I repair to the parlor to receive Mr. A. K. Shriver, who kindly welcomes us to Baltimore, then telephones to Mr. D. J. Foley and other friends. The rest of the party appearing, we all breakfast together.

Mr. Foley is soon presented, and I am cordially impressed with his genial manner, which proclaims at once friendship's sacred charm of sincerity, in the warmth of his happy greeting. His kind blue eyes recall my good mother's gentle features. My heart quickens at sound of his cheery voice, and his felicitous smile is full of winning trustfulness.

Mr. Mark Shriver is next introduced, whom I have mentally photographed as "a man above his kind," a loyal friend, a brave patriot, yet tender hearted as a woman, and I think the picture is true.

They invite us to go upon the roof of the hotel to obtain a bird's-eye view of the city, which we do, and behold the beauteous broad panorama spread before us. The grand sweep of the "blue Patapsco's billowy waves" suggests majesty and power, and the rich splendor of the warm September sun heightens and brightens the vivid scene. Old Fort McHenry, directly east of us, is a relic of the War of 1812, as everybody knows who kens of the circumstances of Francis Scott Key producing that deathless song of the nation, the "Star-spangled Banner," and, strange to remark, to-day is the anniversary of the great fight; flags are flying, processions moving, etc., but for a city the place looks deserted.

After calling attention to each object of interest, the gentlemen conclude that we might return to the lower world, and they kindly accompany us to the cathedral, and tender a history of the ancient pile, with an opportunity to inspect some fine old paintings, two of which were presented to the Baltimore Cathedral by one of the kings of France. The ladies of the Altar Society are in attendance and politely reveal to our admiring eyes the elegant vestments of exquisitely wrought cloth of gold worn by the dignitaries of the church during the council, and other items of lesser interest.

The interior of the cathedral casts a "dim religious light" that seems to softly press the soul to pious prayer. The space around the grand altar has recently been enlarged, and a fine piece of work accomplished overhead in the painting of the transfiguration.

From the edifice we were led to the residence of His Eminence Cardinal Gibbons, and presented to the Primate of America. In the meantime Thos. Foley, Mr. F.'s only son, had joined the party, a handsome young fellow, dark and dangerously fascinating to the young ladies present.

When we were shown into the reception room, His Eminence entered without delay, saluting us most kindly. He is a dignified gentleman, of uncommon magnetic power, a student of rare attainments, whom to see is to love. After a pleasant chat, during which he expressed himself as happy to have received us, he extends his hand in blessing, we each kiss his ring, and take our departure, well pleased with the audience accorded us by His Eminence, through Mr. Foley's thoughtfulness.

Next we visit the German Church of St. Alphonse, which interiorly resembles the cathedral of Boston. Thence we are escorted to the Visitation Convent, where, for the first time in my life, I converse with cloistered nuns. As we await the appearance of Sister Benedicta, sister-in-law of both Mr. Foley and Mr. Shriver, I look curiously about me. The small reception room is partitioned from the hall by iron grating, the first row being iron bars, placed perpendicularly, and about the thickness of inch pipe; the second row is crossbarred. It looks to me the most prison-like place I ever entered.

My surprise is soon broken when a happy nun appears at the double "fencing," and in cheerful tones exclaims: "Now, whom do I know? I'm sure *this* is Fannie Miller!" My start of astonishment is noticed, and I am introduced to Sister Benedicta, who cordially welcomes each in turn, and, with the Rev. Mother's permission, conveys us all through the convent, which I was most desirous of visiting. Sister Benedicta Sanders has been an inmate of this abode of peace for over forty years, during which time she has not been outside of the convent walls, yet, strange as it may seem to my Protestant friends, she is a bright, intelligent, happy woman, a successful teacher, an elocutionist of no mean order, a writer of ability and strength, yet an humble follower of the Master, who promises reward in the present time, and life everlasting hereafter, to those who shall leave home and parents and friends to follow Him. She inquired for Marcella A. Fitzgerald, and sent her messages of love. I expect to call again, and shall enjoy another visit, never yet having been in the atmosphere of learning without feeling its influence.

We return to lunch at the Rennert, and during the afternoon, upon Mr. Shriver's invitation, we take a long, enjoyable drive through the park. Without doubt Druid Hill is the finest park I have seen. Its natural advantages surpass those I have been in—its shady nooks and sunny glades, winding driveways and charming views, quaint old moss-covered trees and fragrant mistletoe, suggestive of Druidic rite, and the extensive green lawn, all cling to the memory in hallowed beauty.

The "Maryland" House of the Centennial has been removed to Druid Hill from Philadelphia, and stands upon an eminence, commanding a picturesque outlook.

Upon our return we enter and inspect the elegant Jenkins Memorial Chapel—a thing of beauty indeed. It is built of gray stone, has valuable insertions of art for windows, an elegantly carved altar, beautiful pictures, and over all an air of perfect finish, which harmonizes the whole. I believe Joseph A. Ford, Esq., is our representative on the coast of the family which has erected this excellent edifice.

Reaching our rooms we prepare for dinner, after which Mr. S. takes Misses Maud and Evie through the market, which they enjoy, and to the candy stores. We retire about eleven, very tired. I write home before retiring.

CHAPTER X.

ROSELAND AND ENNISCORTHY, TYPICAL SOUTHERN HOMES.

Sunday, September 13.

MR. SHRIVER took us to the German Church this morning, after which he got a carriage and drove us to Mrs. Myer's country place, "Roseland," to spend the day. Mrs. Murphy and Martin went to Washington, as the latter is due at Georgetown, and his mother wishes to secure another week's outing for him after entering his name. We all returned in the evening.

"Roseland" is a beautiful spot, about nine miles from town, a typical Southern home, that is always full of gay company, which is hospitably entertained—if we may judge by our own reception. The vast lawn in front of the generous porch is smooth, green, and pretty, edged with blooming rose trees.

Here I met friends whose names are familiar words, Will Myer, for instance, of whom I had heard for years from Mary Foley, and to whom she was afterwards married. I judge him to be a man of thorough integrity, modest in manner, talented, and kind. The young ladies of the household appeared bright and jolly, and fond of society.

After a pleasant day we turned homeward, passing Mt. Hope Retreat, where I have a sick friend, whom I shall call upon ere leaving Maryland.

Monday, September 14.

Mr. Foley called this morning about eleven o'clock, before we had breakfasted, and remained with us almost continuously. He chartered a boat and took us down the river beyond Fort McHenry, accompanied by his son and Mr. Shriver, to view the city from the riverside, and we could ask no greater enjoyment than was afforded in this sail. A brisk, freshening breeze was blowing, and Mr. Foley's hat was swept from his head into the water. The skipper turned his boat and secured the hat with a dipping net. We landlubbers were pleased to place foot on *terra firma* after the unique little voyage.

We next ascended the stairways to the dome of the courthouse, whence we were assured an excellent vista awaited us. We were presented to Mayor Mc———, who, like a new college graduate, seems to feel his weight of honors, and looks perfectly conscious of his new title and position.

We visited the art gallery of Myer, and Hadien's store, then took our lunch, and prepared for a visit to "Enniscorthy," Mr. Foley's country place.

We, as Mr. F.'s guests, took the B. & O. train at Camden Station, reaching Ellicott City in half an hour, and "Enniscorthy," six miles further, in another thirty minutes. The views along the route are truly beautiful; the stone bridges are perfect pictures to me, and the location at Ilchester of the house of the Redemptorist Order is romantic and grand.

We met Mr. Frank Murphy on the train, a delicate-looking, refined young man, connected with the publishing house bearing his familiar name. He is summering at Ilchester.

At "Enniscorthy" we were received by Misses Lillie and Nannie Foley, and their aunt, Miss Sanders, who very cordially greeted us, and hospitably welcomed our coming. Miss Lillie is somewhat tall, with brown eyes and Titian bronze hair, is clever of speech, intellectually bright, with an independent air, and ever a kindly Christian spirit. Miss Nannie is of medium height, fair-haired, with "eyes of most unholy blue," a faultless complexion, sweet in disposition, and the Martha of the household.

Miss Sanders, their gentle aunt, is one of the sweetest characters I ever met, and completes, with "little Josephine," the home circle of "Enniscorthy."

Dinner was announced at six o'clock, and thereafter the evening was most pleasantly beguiled with cards and music. I was charmingly entertained by Miss Lillie with an account of her travels abroad and visit to Oberammergau during the Passion Play. I found her an exceedingly interesting, congenial companion, what Englishmen call "fetching" in appearance, but not particularly pretty—one whom I think to know is to learn from. We felt perfectly at home with these almost new friends, their geniality of manner superinducing that effect.

"Enniscorthy" is in Howard County, and was originally part of the Carroll demense, but purchased some years ago by Mr. Foley as a country summer home for his family, which they called in honor of his birthplace in Wexford, Ireland. The employes are all colored people, excepting the farmer and his family who have charge of the place. The household servants, colored, models of neatness, are systematic in their manner of waiting at table, and graceful as fawns.

As I now prepare to retire, about midnight,

I try to conjecture "what dreams may come," as I am told they may be realized when dreamed under a strange roof.

Tuesday, September 15.

Awakened by the bell, we rise at eight o'clock, breakfast, and walk around the farm. During the outing I find many varieties of fern unlike our native Californians, which I would like to transplant to Miller Hall.

Returning to the house, the carriages await us, and we are driven to Woodstock College, the novitiate of the Jesuits, a most enchanting woodland home, where kind Fr. Sabbetti takes great pride in piloting us through labyrinthian pathways and flower-girt avenues, to inspect gardens and other interesting scenes surrounding the lovely site. Fr. Sabbetti is generous with his floral beauties, and we leave at midday rich with nature's dainty treasures—thoroughly pleased with the drive, and Woodstock charmed.

Reaching "Enniscorthy," we are met by Nannie, whose sweet face, enwreathed in smiles, cheers our way to luncheon, after which lawn tennis and pitchette are indulged in. Lillie invites me for a drive; I accept, and in her cart we speed away to St. Charles Seminary, through which she unceremoniously initiates me, introducing me to Fr. Griffin, then around the grounds, giving snatches of its history as she proceeds. The Sulpicians here and Jesuits at Woodstock evince taste beyond praise in the elegance of their landscape gardening and neatly-arranged pathways and hedges.

From St. Charles we drive to Doughregan Manor, the summer home of the Carroll family, who are now in Europe. The house is in colonial style of architecture, painted white, a veritable home of comfort and beauty.

Handing over our equipage to the care of an aged negro, whom I understand to have been an attaché to the servants' staff of the famous Signer, we wander around to see the conservatory and spacious, neatly-kept lawns, the fine old trees, beautifully-modeled flower plots, and, not least, the handsome chapel, where I note a slab of marble mosaicked into the wall, on the gospel side of the altar inscribed:—

Charles Carroll of Carrollton,
Born Sep. 20th, 1737.
Died Nov. 14th, 1832.

On religious occasions in the slave days the body of this chapel was filled with representatives of the dark race owned by the Carrolls, the pews on each side of the altar being reserved for the family and their friends.

It was a novel sensation to me to kneel and

pray before the altar upon which had been laid the petitions of the brave hero who erected this shrine and was equally faithful to his country and his God.

The shades of gloaming warn us of the necessity of returning. We find the party at "Enniscorthy" engaged in a game of croquet, which occupies the moments "'tween the gloamin' and the murk," until dinner, after which we enjoy the calm evening on the porch, and cards in the drawing room. Miss Lillie grouped us for a picture and kodaked us by flash light.

We retire with the memory of a very delightful day to soothe our eyes to slumber.

CHAPTER XI.

SCENES IN GETTYSBURG.

Wednesday, September 16.

WE left the lovely scenes of "Enniscorthy" this morning to take train for Baltimore, to keep an engagement with two friends. Driving with Messrs. Foley, Jr., and Shriver to Ellicott City, heartily imbibing the fresh air, enjoying the hush of the morning stillness, we reached our station in time, but the train was late. We arrived in Baltimore at 10:30. While awaiting my friends, I occupied the interim writing to the dear ones at home an account of my stay at Mr. Foley's.

I lunched with friends and enjoyed the fish menu very much. My cousins joined me later. We then went for a drive over Crimea Hill, a sequestered, picturesque driveway, resembling our Marin County mountain roads, through an almost primeval forest, where I secured some ferns to send home. After dinner several friends came to spend the evening with us, whose society we enjoyed. Retire late, very weary.

Thursday, September 17.

Accompanying a friend, and armed with a letter of introduction to Sr. Catherine, Superior at Mt. Hope, from Mr. Foley, I start for the Retreat, on the train. In twenty-five minutes we whirl into the station, at the hospital, where we have an invalid friend, whom I am desirous of seeing ere leaving Baltimore, and have taken occasion to call to-day. After spending a couple of hours within the solitudes of this saddening place, we returned, reaching the Rennert at midday.

After lunch we prepare for a trip, tendered us by Mr. Shriver, and at 3:30 leave for Gettysburg *via* the Western Maryland Railroad, arriving in the famous battle burg at 7:30. Here we are lodged at the City Hotel, the best the place affords, conducted by a man as capacious of build and size as John L. Sullivan. His voice is as sonorous as the western wind, and he glibly assigns the ladies to two rooms, which boast four couches, with the assurance to Evie that if she rolls out of the window her fall will be broken by a roof several feet below—very comfortable sensations to sleep on.

Mrs. Murphy, Maud, and Mr. Tom Foley have just returned from up town, where our chaperon laid in her usual supply of souvenir *cucharas.* She presented me with a lovely orange spoon. I note its characteristics, kiss the donor, and place it with my beauteous collection, the gift of the same generous soul.

Friday, September 18.

After breakfasting, we wander about until ten o'clock, when the large, convenient carryall secured by our entertainer is brought up, and we seat ourselves within its comfortable space to view the scenes of the bravely-fought battle that was "to decide the fate of human liberty." It is a very warm, sunny day, but the ride is most agreeable, over the ground of the first day's contest. To our left, on the south side, as we drive over Chambersburg turnpike, is seen Cemetery Ridge, and farther still Culp's Hill, which Longstreet was aiming to possess. Near at hand, on our right, is a yellow building, the Seminary, from the cupola of which General Buford took observations of the surrounding country. It gives the name Seminary Ridge to the elevation upon which it stands.

Taking a northerly direction from the turnpike to an avenue, on our right is shown the line of battle, the position of the Federal troops being commemorated by a row of stately monuments, white marble, granite, and other valuable stone and bronze predominating. Each handsomely-wrought design signifies where regiments were stationed. They were placed there either by the State to which the regiments belonged, or by the surviving comrades, under the auspices of the "Battlefield Memorial Association." Over the scene of cruel carnage, thirty miles square, there are already four hundred of these majestic memorials, with many more in course of completion. One Confederate shaft was permitted to be placed. It was done by the State of Maryland.

They are too numerous for me to particularize, but I may remark the spot where General Reynolds was killed, whereon, in heavy gray granite, is told the tale of his fall, supposed to have been a shot from an ambushed sharpshooter, which struck him in the eye and passed out over his left temple. He fell from his horse and his neck was broken.

We pass along, reading and inspecting monuments, until our eyes are weary with the white glare of sunshine on the marble. We halt at the spring where General Lee's soldiers lay sick on the second day's battle, from drinking the waters, which were supposed to have been poisoned. To us it tasted of magnesia and soda. Little wonder that the poor fellows became ill, in the scorching heat of July's raging sun, and the added warmth of desperate conflict.

Making the circuit, we return to the town about noon, having pleasantly and instructively spent a forenoon of intense interest. Wandering around, I make inquiries respecting the place, and am informed that the present site of Gettysburg was originally the property of Wm. Penn, but about 1780 came into the possession of a man named Gettys, who divided it into town lots, and called it after himself, "Gettysburg." Entering the "Antiquarian Store" we are shown many curios, most of which have been picked up on the field, among them a Confederate and a Federal bullet which met in the air and were welded, by the force, into one.

Returning to the hotel we lunch and prepare for the afternoon's excursion. Mr. Herbert Shriver, of Union Mills, and Mr. Brown, of Philadelphia, drive up to spend the day with us, and after lunch join us in the coach, when, with a competent guide, Mr. Minnock, we start off to inspect Cemetery Ridge and the entire stage whereon was enacted one of the most bloody dramas of the war. It is a grand excursion, full of revelation, instructive and beautiful.

Attention is directed to the house wherein Jennie Wade was killed by a shell while making bread. We soon reach the cemetery. It is divided in the center by a long, shady lane.

On the left, as we approach, are interred the civilians, the right side being reserved for the military graves, where lie hundreds of soldiers, many of them with blank slabs marking the mound, unknown, but of course not unwept. A New York State monument calls attention, being ninety-two feet high and costing $5,000.

The cemetery is designed in a semicircle running north and south, with the elegant national monument in the center, fashioned after the Immaculate Conception Monument in Rome, surmounted by the Goddess of Liberty, and four handsome figures around the pedestal representing *Peace* (a mechanic), *War* (a U. S. soldier), *History* (a woman sitting with open scroll in her hand), and *Plenty* (a woman with sheaves of wheat).

We drive through the avenue, and alight from our carriage to walk up Cemetery Hill, listening as the guide recites the story, in pathetic, aye, poetic language, of the cruel strife. He points out the almshouse, which we had seen in the morning, and mentions young Wilkinson, who amputated his own shattered limb with his sword, dragged himself to the almshouse, used as a hospital, but died next morning, after a night of insufferable pain.

The Blue Ridge Mountains, in cerulean tint, line the western horizon, and the valley of the

Cumberland stretches beyond them. The broad battle ground, mapped in nature's lines, lies before us. The charges made and their location are all carefully rehearsed. The breastworks thrown up are still at our feet, lessened and rounded by time. Cannons rest here and there, their brazen mouths closed, their deadly work done. The dauntless "Louisiana Tigers," under Hays, here did splendid work, but, laboring under great disadvantages, were finally repulsed. It is recorded that on this spot was fought one of the most frenzied hand-to-hand struggles of the three days' carnage. Culp's Hill stands serenely to the southeast, in wooded beauty and unforgotten glory.

We reënter the vehicle, and, following the Emmitsburg Pike, are shown the scene, on our right, of "Pickett's Charge," the great and marvelous piece of determined bravery of the war. Gallantly charging the Union lines across a field a mile broad, under a hurricane of shot and shell, the brave column swept grandly onward, until mowed down in its advance by the withering blast of belching musketry concentrated on its chivalrous front. The repulse was complete, and but a handful of men who participated in this fearful attack survived.

Passing by the peach orchard mentioned in history, which has been twice planted since the war, we come to grain fields, and finally are wending our way over the serpentine road of Culp's Hill, whence we are soon led into the "Devil's Den," a wild, tumbled lot of bowlders, evidently massed by a convulsion of nature, with a crystalline stream issuing from their cavernous depths. Dismounting we view the uncanny spot with curiosity. It was an excellent cover for the lurking sharpshooter, and our guide informs us that among the clump of rocks fell many wounded soldiers, who lay undiscovered for days. He showed us where the bones of a Georgia soldier still lie, a kindly hand having lately covered them with earth.

Barefooted, ragged children emerge from the broken débris with cupfuls of the clear water, which they offer—not in His name—but for the material reward cheerfully granted by the bevy of visitors, who feel the effects of September's ardent sun

Pursuing our way towards the Round Tops, over a beautifully designed road shaded by oak and hickory trees, we suddenly appear before a large Irish cross in granite, with the Irish wolf lying at its base, in bronze, the monument of the "69th Irish Regiment," marking the place where mass was said for the regiment before the second day's battle, when, as the priest raised his hand in blessing on the kneeling soldiers, the word, "Forward!" came from General Kelly, and instantly ranks were formed, and the men in battle line, ready for action. I am proud of my Irish and my Faith!

The roadway leads to Spangler's Springs, and we drink of the water that supplied both armies with refreshment during the contest. Round Top reached we again alight, and view the vast, graveyard-like valley, bristling with shafts of marble and granite.

Here Mr. Minnock explains the movements and incidents of the second and third days' battles, interesting to hear, but not readily understood by one possessed of as limited knowledge of warfare as I may claim. The trees hereabouts, scarred and bullet-wounded, show the effects of the hot fire poured into their midst, some lying prone upon the ground, falling to decay, shelled by enemies not their own. On Little Round Top I note a life-size figure in bronze of General Warren, who saved the "Round Tops."

Descending to the flat country we follow the stone wall road to a spot hallowed by a scroll of marble, where General Hancock anxiously kept watch of the day's movements and vicissitudes, directing his men, without once losing patience. This is near what is termed "the bloody angle," when the third day's battle swept out regiments of the confederacy, every inch of the air being black with the winged missiles of death. The battle closed on the 4th of July, 1863, after three days of mortal strife. General Lee, than whom no braver soldier held a sword, disheartened and discouraged, withdrew beyond the distant Blue Ridge, and passed a wretched night and day in sadness, his men sick, weary, and footsore.

Now, my diary, there is much that I could not sufficiently grasp to properly place in your keeping, and mayhaps I have become wearisome relating what everybody—but myself—already knew. However, as I never saw the "Panorama of Gettysburg," and never had entertained an idea of the magnitude of the battle until now, I may be excused for jotting down the items that arrested my interest.

Returning *via* Hancock Avenue to Gettysberg, we dine at the City Hotel, and Mr. Shriver provides two carriages for our conveyance to Emmittsburg, which ancient little city we set out for at 6:30 P. M. We arrive in Emmittsburg, ten miles distant, about nine o'clock, and are booked at a hotel *sans* name, managed on rather primitive plans. Retiring about ten o'clock, very tired, we gladly welcome balmy sleep.

CHAPTER XII.

THE CITY OF EMMITTSBURG; THE OLD HOMESTEAD AT "UNION MILLS."

September 19.

RISING with the break of dawn, and breakfasting early, we are free to stroll about and see the peculiarities of the town. It is an old-fashioned, quiet place. The people are lazy-looking, and the streets are dirty and much in need of sidewalks. The stores are like the little country shops of suburban towns in California. The houses look old, many of them dilapidated, and the hotel fare is miserable.

Mr. Shriver's sister-in-law, with her son and daughter, call to see us, and conduct us to the Convent of St. Euphemia, near the parish church, to see some of its inmates who are Californians. They are delighted to see us, and truly royal in their earnest welcome to pilgrims from the West. They accompanied us to Mt. St. Joseph's, founded in 1815 by Mother Seton, and the entire building was thrown open for our inspection.

Our admiration of the elegant convent, a retreat of repose, embowered by majestic trees, in the heart of a broad green lawn, is indeed beyond expression. Its health-giving resources, large, excellently ventilated rooms, spacious grounds, beautiful gardens, with perfect cleanliness and order throughout, are attractions to which we yield unbounded homage. The chapel is exquisite in its finish and furnishings. A beautiful shrine in the garden marks the resting place of Mother Seton, and beside her have been placed the remains of the late Archbishop Bailey, her kinsman. Near by is the house she erected, where she lived, taught, led others to life everlasting, and died. Mr. Shriver's mother, now aged eighty-three, is one of the original fifteen pupils taught in this small schoolhouse, by Mother Seton, in 1815.

Bidding adieu to our gentle friends, we are taken by our host to Mt. St. Mary's Seminary and College, where Fr. Allen is pastor and Superior. The drive hither is pleasant and the approach to the college beautiful. It is the institution which has reared the most gigantic minds in American church history, and I am happy to be privileged to inspect it. The paintings are ancient and elegant, the college of a superior standard of learning, and its situation romantic and isolated, on a hillside covered with evergreen shrubbery and beautiful trees. Registering in the President's Visitors' Book, after a tour through the halls and grounds of the old college, we take our course towards "Haylands," the home of Mr. Wm. Shriver.

A short distance from Mt. St. Mary's, I note "Clearlands," the old home of the Shorb family. The house, constructed of gray stone, low in stature, homelike in appearance, stands upon a knoll in bold command of a complete view of "Emmittsburg" and the surrounding country. Weed-grown and neglected, the old home and birthplace of chivalrous Dr. Shorb, one of California's favorite adopted sons, rests firmly on its foundations. Its once-honored inmates have passed away; old associations have vanished; the music of their joy is hushed forever, yet the staunch, enduring stone remaineth.

At "Haylands" we lunch, spend a pleasant hour, then hasten to the train for Westminster, *en route* for "Union Mills." Traveling through part of Pennsylvania, the trip is enjoyable and the route pretty. Quaintly-attired Quakers board the cars, carrying baskets of flowers and fruit.

With evening's lengthening shadows we reach Westminster, and from the depot are conveyed in carriages to "Union Mills," six miles distant. On the train from Baltimore

Mr. Herbert Shriver was accompanied by Rev. Fr. Grannan, professor of philosophy at the Catholic University of Washington, who is coming to "the Mills" for the purpose of conducting religious service in the private chapel of the Shriver family.

About dusk we arrive in sight of the old homestead, and I mark the air of restful comfort which invites one to repose and peace within the sweet precincts of hospitality's arms, spread open over scenes as fresh and fair as morning's face. At the gate we are greeted by the Misses Shriver and their venerable lady mother, who has the soft, low voice that poets love. Gently inviting us to remove our hats and wraps, we are led to rooms that repeat the atmosphere of ease everywhere breathed in this charming home.

Dinner is soon announced, and the dining hall fills with guests, ready to enjoy a most generous and delicious menu, and each other's genial society. The meal concluded we are accompanied across the turnpike to the mill race, and treated to a most romantic and enjoyable boat sail. Stepping into the little shallop from a picturesque, rustic bridge, spanning the stream 'neath the umbrageous branches of a weeping willow, we are rowed by master hands in the art, up the winding rivulet, cheered by voices in sweet song. It is a beautiful evening, and as we glide along, round curves and shallows, the spirit of merriment rules the hour. Right here Evie thought she had encountered her *kismet*, but there was "a difference in the morning"!

As we stroll back to the house of our hostess, I inquire about it, and the reason of the title "Union Mills," and am informed that the ancestors of the possessors of this property obtained it in 1797, engaging in the milling business, and by united exertion in the management of flour and grist mills and a successful sawmill, they designated their combined property as "Union Mills," which name is retained. The home of our entertainers was built in 1828, and is a commodious dwelling, located near the turnpike, and almost encompassed by neatly-cropped lawns and selected shade trees, among which I was shown a specimen of the mahogany, the only one I have ever seen.

Retiring about eleven, I enjoy somnolent repose, my mind replete with "a picture on the brain."

Sunday, September 20.

At half past seven we are in the prayer-inspiriting little chapel, attending the divine office, celebrated by Fr. Grannan, being served by Mr. Herbert Shriver and his little son Joseph, whose grandmother walked up to the railing to receive the blessed sacrament as spryly as the young people, although eighty-three winters have left their snows upon her head.

The holy services ended, we repair to the breakfast room for our morning meal, and discuss an excellent repast. Enjoying the lovely day we saunter about, and climb the lawn-covered slope to "Avalon," the home of Mr. B. F. Shriver, and are introduced to his interesting family. Glancing down from the porch of his handsome residence, a fine sweep of country is overseen, with a living stream meandering through the center, which I am told is Big Pipe Creek, so called from the custom of the Indians to smoke the calumet on its banks. A stroll "down by the old mill stream," another cheery row on its sparkling waters, and the hours roll on to midday, when we lunch.

Another outing directs our wanderings to a substantial stone bridge over the creek, whose graceful arches mirrored in the stream claim my longing wish to sketch, and what a pretty picture I would have! This bridge was constructed in 1807, and has nobly withstood storm and tempest for more than eighty years.

We were initiated into the mysteries of milling flour, which is an interesting process, but, although a *Miller born* myself, I am not competent of penning the result of to-day's schooling in the art which causes man to appreciate the moisture "of his brow."

I have been feeling ill all this afternoon, my old annoyance, neuralgia, troubling me, so I seek the charms of repose. Mr. A. K. Shriver took the party out driving, and they express great delight and pleasure with the cruise of enjoyment afforded them.

At four o'clock P. M. we attended benediction of the Blessed Sacrament, given by Fr. Grennan, and the remainder of the day passes pleasantly away. Maud, spicily amusing herself with a callow youth from across the pike, is an audible goddess of laughter—was there ever another? Evalyn is engaged with me, admiring the exquisite handicraft of Miss Mollie Shriver, beautifully enwrought on the altar cloths, vestments, and other articles belonging to the chapel, which evinces the devout spirit of the gentle toiler whose fair hands accomplished all this dainty artistic work. After tea, which is indeed supper, we repair to the parlor, bidding moments speed on the wings of sweet harmony. Nearing the witching hour o' midnight we claim Morpheus as our king.

Monday, September 21.

After hearing mass celebrated for a deceased

member of the family, we breakfasted, bade *adios* to the kind, hospitable friends of "Union Mills," whose voices in our "echoing hearts a sound must long remain," and take carriages for Westminster, to meet the Baltimore train, Fr. Grennan accompanying us.

Rolling into Baltimore at eleven o'clock, we soon meet Messrs. Foley, Senior and Junior, who kindly come to hail our return, and with them we do a round of shopping, lunching at the Rennert, and at 4:45 take the train for Washington, D. C. Over an excellently balanced road we rapidly speed, snatching glimpses of wood-embossed valleys, dimpled hills, and brawling streams, and reaching Washington at 6:30 P. M., as the gray curtains of dusk begin to droop.

Taking apartments at the Arlington, a splendid hotel, we are again satisfactorily situated, and prepare to acknowledge a bevy of letters from home, which anticipated our arrival.

CHAPTER XIII.

MOUNT VERNON.

Tuesday, September 22.

THIS morning, at ten o'clock, we board the *Chas. McAlester*, a pretty little steamer that floats down the Potomac like a bird, for Mt. Vernon. The day is extremely warm, yet we imbibe the beauty of the scenery on both banks of the river, over which hangs in dreamy languor, a glamour of soft haze. At 11:30 Mt. Vernon heights are seen, and we set foot on the landing, canopied, and beautified by Mrs. Hearst, the Regent for California.

Pursuing our way up the slope, we reach the tomb of our first President, and reverently note its most salient characteristics; thence, following the path, we inspect the mansion, the rooms and furniture, so patriotically reclaimed from the ruining possession of idle time by the stout-hearted women of America.

The view from the veranda of the mansion is a picture for Bierstadt's brush. The blue waters of the almost national river sweep smoothly by, bearing stately vessels on their tide, that salute with flying flag and tolling bell this site of beauty and renown. The mental impulse to indulge in dreamy retrospective pleasure is peculiarly strong when standing upon the ground where lived and died the noble hero of American history, who gazed upon the charming scenes we now view admiringly, and with sincere desire to preserve in the "amber of memory." Mrs. Murphy had our group photographed on the lawn, with the mansion for a background. It is a neat souvenir of the lovely place.

Leaving Mt. Vernon at 1:30 we steam up the river, passing by Alexandria, the "city of ruins," where we are shown the house wherein Colonel Ellsworth, the first victim of the Rebellion, was killed; also old Christ Church, in which Washington was vestryman. I must note that in Alexandria Washington cast his first vote, in 1754, and his last, in 1799. It is a city of memories, for "'tis a city of ruins."

As we approach the metropolis, the Washington Monument, standing in its towering might of five hundred and fifty-five feet, looks majestic and grand, reflected for a mile in the dimpling waters of the Potomac. The capitol also is an imposing structure seen from the river.

Having lunched on the boat, a miserable meal, we have time to drive around the city and shop. Evie is ailing under the oppressive heat of the day. Martin and Maud attend the theater.

Wednesday, September 23.

Accompanied Mrs. M. on a shopping tour, and then to Georgetown College, to leave Martin. The town is not a particularly pretty place, the university being perhaps the chief building of prominence, and I am told it is the object which gives the town note. It is a handsome gray stone structure, formidable-looking and somewhat suggestive of pictures I have seen of the new Catholic university, which I expect to view later. Fr. Richards took us all through the fine establishment, and we obtained a pretty view of Virginia across the river, Arlington Heights, formerly the Lee plantation, Roselands, and the monument, etc., etc. Georgetown is now called Western Washington, so closely does it hug the once more distant city.

Driving back to W, we find several friends at the hotel awaiting us. After dinner with them, they escort us for a walk, showing us the different public buildings, etc.

Thursday, September 24.

The Messrs. H. and A. K. Shriver called this

morning, and, having secured a three-seated carriage, drove us to the Soldiers' Home and Catholic university, around by Ecklands, which was an excursion of most pleasing reminiscences. At the university we were presented to Bishop Keane, the "silver-tongued orator" of the Catholic pulpit. He is a man of most attractive address, and with whom I am particularly charmed. Here, too, we met Fr. Grannan, who kindly afforded us the pleasure of an insight of the elegant college interior throughout—a privilege enjoyed through our escorts, Dr. Grannan's friends, and for which we are deeply indebted. The magnificent buildings stand on a high knoll in bold relief, trees girting the base of the eminence, and the broad front of the massive structure is almost as enduring in strength as the truths taught within its granite walls.

After lunching at the Arlington, I was invited to see the Botanical Gardens and Smithsonian Institute, all of which I heartily enjoyed. After dinner we all went for a walk, and Mr. S. left for Baltimore on an evening train.

CHAPTER XIV.

THE CAPITOL AT WASHINGTON.

September 25.

AFTER our matutinal meal, we call for a carriage and go to the capitol, hire a guide, and see the entire interior of the wonderful building, the paintings, frescoing, and statuary, all of a high order of art. In the old Hall of Representatives stands Vinnie Ream's statue of Lincoln, for which the talented little woman received from the government ten thousand dollars. It is a fine piece of work. Bierstadt's picture of Monterey is not up to my idea of the artist's possibilities. Henry Hudson discovering the river is a finely conceived poem on canvas. The large fresco piece " Westward the Course of Empire Takes Its Way," illustrating the rugged road to California in 1848, is excellent. The Golden Gate beneath, with dear old Marin's rocky cliffs projecting over their water-washed base, is familiar as sunlight.

The United States Senate chamber is very handsome, and the United States Supreme

Court room is plainer but serious looking. The President's room, where he signs the bills passed by Congress, is especially beautiful, the frescoing elegant. The lobby is interesting, and, oh, if its walls could speak! We tried the acoustic properties of the old Hall of Representatives, where stands Franzoni's clock, and were interested and amused. Next we visited the "Gold Room," where the speaker of the House receives his friends. The lobby here is lined with portraits of ex-speakers, most prominent of whom is James G. Blaine.

The rotunda regained we pass out. Immediately in the center of the rotunda is a bit of white marble, marking the spot where is placed in state the bier holding the remains of the nation's honored dead. Here rested the pall of Lincoln, Garfield, Grant, and others.

Leaving the capitol, we take our way to the Monument and ascend in the elevator to the summit, five hundred feet; the other fifty-five feet are above us. This monument was eleven years building. It stands on the Potomac's edge and commands a matchless view of the river. In the elevator were about thirty persons, and we were nearly smothered in the crowd, being as closely packed as sardines in a can.

Visiting the Corcoran Art Gallery, I was delighted to see an original Paul Veronese, representing a scene in the "Passion of Christ." I enjoyed the handsome pictures and statuary groups very much.

I feel very tired and ill, possibly the result of the sultry weather and unusual walking indoors, which is wearisome to me. Received letters from home, which, of course, were like dear friends' faces, welcome and pleasing.

Saturday, September 26.

Am very uncomfortable to-day; the sultry warmth is exceedingly depressing, and a feverish, malarial feeling, most unwelcome, to say the least, is asserting itself. Rousing myself from the languorous influence, I go out shopping with Mrs. Murphy, and purchase gifts for my California friends. My cousin friend selects Mt. Vernon and Washington spoons, that are art studies of beauty, and with the late addition of Baltimore, Enniscorthy, and Union Mills souvenir spoons, my collection from Mrs. Murphy is constantly enlarging.

Returned to the Arlington overheated and ailing. On an evening train from Baltimore Mr. A. K. Shriver arrived, and after dinner took Misses Maud and Evie and myself for a jaunt through the park, through the grounds of the White House, and elsewhere. Martin attended his mother on her return from the college and gayly greets us as we enter the hotel. He is enthusiastic in praise of Georgetown, and I think will take due advantage of the opportunity here afforded towards a liberal education. Now a care-free, good-hearted, unaffectedly humorous young man, the outlook of his future is excellent under the régime of Georgetown, after which there is much to be expected.

Sunday, September 27.

We all attend mass at St. Matthew's Church, Rev. Dr. Chappelle, the bishop elect of Albuquerque, New Mexico, offering up the Holy Sacrifice, and preaching a farewell sermon to his flock, during which he is tearfully affected. For the first time since leaving California Maud succumbs to climatic influence, and almost faints in church. It is very warm and sunny.

At nine o'clock we take our breakfast, and retire to our rooms to write letters, Mr. S. leaving for Baltimore, and the happy "tease," Martin, returning to Georgetown. The oppressive heat has almost prostrated me. Am unable to withstand much heat, having once been partially sunstruck.

Mrs. Edward Martin, of California, is at this hotel with her sons, students of Georgetown.

After an outing we retire, with our windows

wide agape, mosquitoes lively and hungry, and the air heavy and hot. We find rest a wishedfor thing with which we are not to be blessed.

Monday, September 28.

After returning from the breakfast room I feel indisposed and unrefreshed. Dr. Wales— beg pardon, no kinsman to the prince—has been sent for, and his orders are for rest and sleep, neither of which I may justly claim while traveling. However, I remain for the day in my room, as close as I can reach his advice. Am very much fatigued, the effects of immoderate walking, to which I am a stranger. At noon Mr. Shriver came over from Baltimore, bringing us letters. Evening finds us packing for home.

To-day Mrs. M. and Maud attended the President's reception. It continues sultry and sickening. During the calm of twilight Mr. Shriver took Evie and myself for a drive and kindly introduced us to parts of the city with a view of which we had not before been favored.

The Chinese Legation, and mansions of the British and French Legations, with others, and the fire-ruined house of Secretary Tracy, wherein his wife perished, the house of interesting history occupied by Mr. Blaine, and innumerable others were shown us, with a thousand objects of remark and interest. The bronze figures of our national heroes adorning every available space of ground stand out in bold relief 'twixt our vision and the opaline sky.

The evening was lovely. The delightful outing ended, we retraced our course, to regain our rooms for early rest.

CHAPTER XV.

LAST DAYS IN MARYLAND.

Tuesday, September 29.

HAVE had no sleep, and but little rest all night. I am pleased that it is our last day in Washington, which handsome city I have been able to only dreamily enjoy, the enervating climate having deprived me of all energy and spirit to mingle in scenes around which the enchantment of interest revolves.

We take leave of Martin, who keeps bravely up in parting with his loved ones. Our belongings having been forwarded to the depot, Mr. Shriver takes charge of the party and accompanies us to Baltimore, where we are to take the afternoon train on our homeward-bound trip. The Rennert is gained about noon. I feel wretchedly ill, alternately feverish and chilly, and *cross as a bear.* I'm sure everybody will know that I am a "native daughter of the Golden West." Our Baltimore friends called to wish us Godspeed and prevailed in soft persuasion to postpone our departure until the morrow. Mr. Shriver and Mr. Tom Foley tendered us "a spin" through the park, which was exceedingly pleasant to those feeling well and bright.

Having accepted Mrs. Mark Shriver's invitation to tea, and to spend the evening in her sweet home of domestic bliss, thither we repaired as the dusky brow of eventide began to lower. A warm welcome from the kindliest hearts in Baltimore, and the evening's pleasure was assured. With my dear favorite, old Horace, I sincerely believe that nothing on this earth can "with a true, genial friend compare," and such I take our host to be, and his lovely, amiable, dark-eyed wife. After the prettily-served supper, Mr. Foley escorted Misses Maud and Evie to the theater, and the rest sped the winging hours with cards.

During the evening Mr. C. C. Shriver and his charming wife, formerly Miss Paine, of Virginia, dropped in, and in the opportunity offered to become acquainted through conversational influence with her admirable character, I did not regret the awkwardness of card handling that kept me from joining the players tonight.

With the waning hour towards midnight we betook ourselves hotelward, and, in parting, the refrain of Moore, so full of sentiment, welled upward from my heart:—

"Farewell! but whenever you welcome the hour
That awakens the night song of mirth in your bower,
Then think of the friend who once welcom'd it too,
And forgot his own griefs to be happy with you."

Wednesday, September 30.

With the first burst of daylight I am up and about. Mr. Foley and Miss Lillie called, having traveled from "Enniscorthy" this morning. Upon invitation I accompany them to their city house, through which Lillie leads me to inspect the comfortably-planned, elegantly-furnished home, whose solid joys keep happy the winter and spring months of the year, the summer and autumn calling its cherished inmates to the sea of greenery swelling and encompassing sweet "Enniscorthy."

We return for breakfast at eleven o'clock, after which Miss Lillie and Mr. Charlie Murphy, of Baltimore, take us to visit the Johns Hopkins Hospital, a munificently endowed institution for the needy, and conducted on plans of magnificent liberality. Of the staff of physicians in charge, Dr. Osler, a refined-looking, entertaining gentleman, politely attends us through the beautifully-kept dormitories, wards, halls, and rooms, and throughout I note with inquisitive glance all modern improvements and convenient appurtenances, with a ventilating system peculiarly its own. Rooms of superior comfort are reserved for those able to pay. The staff of nurses is not excelled in America; nearly all are young, strong, healthy-looking girls, under the care and direction of a competent matron. The hospital is the gift of Johns Hopkins, a worthy and creditable philanthropist of Baltimore, who died about eight years ago, and is now designated as "St. Johns Hopkins" by his admiring friends.

The memorial room is fittingly furnished with his own belongings. Particularly attractive is a long, expensive, massively-carved black table, with six legs, placed in the center of the room. Bric-a-brac, rich and rare, adorn the walls, and from this room one carries away a unique impression.

The Nurses' Home adjoins the hospital buildings, and we were permitted a peep into the matron's apartments, which bespeak the characteristics of the occupant, respectability and strict sense of discipline everywhere discernible. The genial Dr. Osler cunningly invited us to join the force of nurses, and, as inducement, admitted that one of the most aristocratic members of the medical staff had lately married one of the trained nurses—inducement enough, and promotion.

I am gratified with the pleasure afforded by this visit to the Hopkins Hospital, and have enjoyed it thoroughly. Reaching the hotel, we find Mrs. Frank Smith, a friend of Miss Foley's, who has called to meet us, on Lillie's invitation. She is a gentle, suave lady, refined and kind. Mr. Herbert Shriver and his children also greet us, soon followed by Mr. Foley, and Messrs. Al. Myer and Tom Foley. At 1:30 we accept Mr. A. K. Shriver's invitation to lunch, and at table form an interesting group.

At 2:30 we drive to the B. & O. R. R Depot, and sorrowfully say farewell to the dear friends who have been so hospitable and kind during our stay in their midst. Mr. Shriver, however, takes advantage of our westward course to make a business trip to St. Louis, and we are delighted, having found, too, the need of a man a distressing reality.

Turning from Baltimore we run into Washington, remaining fifteen or twenty minutes, then steam directly west, *en route* for Cincinnati. About eighty miles from Baltimore, along the Potomac and its canal, we come to the oft-heard-of Harper's Ferry, and cross the Potomac at its junction with the Shenandoah. The Blue Ridge drags its length to the eastward. The peak of Jefferson's Rock, where the noble statesman harangued the people, to the left, almost overhangs old "John Brown's Fort," and the village which was once the place for manufacturing arms, etc., for the government. The "Fort" is a small brick house and is not formidable-looking, yet I suppose has served its purpose. Stonewall Jackson's position on the bluff holding possession of the valley is proudly indicated, when General Banks was driven back in slaughter. The arsenal was burned, of course, but its foundation remains, ruined and worthless.

The broad valley of Virginia stretches between the Blue Ridge and Alleghanies, in places thirty miles in extent, and is a beautiful, wooded, fertile country, fully recovered from the results of the army inroads thirty years ago. It runs south, or to the left of us, and the Cumberland sweeps to the north 'neath the shadow of the Blue Ridge. Winding along the south bank of the Potomac, we pass through and witness scenery as boldly grand and picturesque as may be found in any part of Switzerland, or other boasted scenic country of Europe.

West Virginia is now to be seen at its best. The scarlet leaves of the dogwood are being retouched by nature's brush, and other brilliant foliage charms the sight and claims the admiration of nature's lovers of the beautiful.

The reflection of mountains, trees, blossomed bushes, and tangled shrubbery in the clear streams is enchanting—almost ideal. War-noted hamlets, among which is Martinsburg, are being indicated by Mr. Shriver, who is familiar with the country hereabout.

As twilight settles upon the silent waters of the river, it tips its softly-flowing ripples with silver and throws the tree shadows in darker relief, and still we skurry along at tremendous rate, halting but a moment at intervening stations between Harper's Ferry and Cumberland, a distance of one hundred miles. Cumberland, the queen city of the Alleghanies, is very prettily nestled in the heart of the mountains, but the darkening night clouds nearly conceal its beauties. The Narrows suggest the Colorado Gorge, and Deer Park is brilliantly ablaze with electric light. Garrett's Cottage, wherein Mr. Cleveland spent his honeymoon with his lovely bride, is a feature of the place. I regret that the afterglow of sunset has faded, evening has merged into night, and I must retire without further view of this exquisite picture on nature's own canvas, which I so much enjoy.

CHAPTER XVI.

HOMEWARD BOUND.

Thursday, October 1.

RESTLESS and unrefreshed, I am wearily dull. We crossed the Ohio River near Marietta during the "wee sma' hours of the dawn," and reached Cincinnati at 7:30, but could not remain long, so boarded the Ohio and Mississippi train for Louisville, Kentucky. Coursing along the banks of the Ohio, with Kentucky on our left, we pass into Indiana and find that sameness in the scenery which wearies, although it is a beautiful, richly-endowed country. At North Vernon, Indiana, we take a direct course southward to Louisville. It is quite warm, but pleasant.

Cincinnati is a business breathing city; its people are active, and commendably attentive to their own affairs. The sandy banks of the Ohio, with its slow-moving waters on our left, is spanned by two immense railroad bridges, one leading to Covington, Kentucky, the other taking us along the road to Louisville. We recross the Ohio near the latter city, and for the first time I see canal locks and am shown how they operate, the Ohio River having a canal here that is kept in order, the river proper being liable to change.

We arrive in Louisville at high noon, and register at Louisville Hotel. The town is literally alive with people, who are celebrating the Harvest Festival with processions, balls, fairs, etc. The prettiest women and handsomest men I have yet seen are in this city. To-night they are crowding the hotel, and the streets are lined with people.

We took a carriage to-day and went wherever fancy suggested. Drove down the fine thoroughfare called Broadway, where we noted handsome residences, also saw the new custom house, and the handsome Union Depot. Drove into and around Mr. Dupont's private park, a tame, old-fashioned looking place. In all the city have only seen *two* superior teams of carriage horses, whereas I looked for fine horses *everywhere* in Kentucky. Mules there are without number or character, with darkies as Jehus in every instance.

We take supper, and at eight o'clock start for St. Louis on the O. & M., sleeping on the train.

Friday, October 2.

Upon arriving at St. Louis we were taken directly to the Southern Hotel. After some delay Mr. S. succeeded in securing rooms, although every one had been engaged, it being the carnival week, and fête of the Veiled Prophet. The hotel is now said to be absolutely fireproof, and is carried on on the American plan, It is thronged with guests. The city is elegantly illuminated. Broadway Street is lit up in half circles across the thoroughfare, and others have lamps within globes for a stretch of seven miles, giving an enchantingly beautiful effect·

During the forenoon we rested. Early in the afternoon Miss O'Meara and Miss Taylor, with her brother, called to arrange for a drive. I decline to go, as my malarial tendency is again troubling me, and I prefer to follow the doctor's orders and try to rest. In the evening we all attend the Royal Arcanum Society's Concert, by Gilmore's Band, a charitable institution for the benefit of widows and orphans. Some of the music is of a high order, and the songs by the male quartette are very fine. We returned early, to seek needed repose.

Saturday, October 3.

Misses O'Meara and Taylor called to guide us around town, and conducted us to the public library, a well-filled establishment of select reading matter splendidly arranged, under the superintendence of Mr. Anderson, a scholarly man, with literary taste. A superbly carved figure in wood of Robert Burns, with four of his best poems illustrated on the pedestal, is a unique piece of art I particularly admired in one corner of a room adjoining the library. Other fine art treasures belong here, and some valuable canvases are stored on its walls.

Jewelry stores are next visited for souvenir spoons, and, as usual, Mrs. Murphy favors me with another. My friends are about to attend the matinee, so I return to the Southern, to await their coming to dinner at five.

In the meantime I take an outing in the park. A life-size statue of Frank Blair, who saved Missouri from secession, stands at the entrance. The park is a pretty driveway, and does not seem as large as I am told it is, being second to Fairmount in size. Druid Hill is still my favorite.

We dined at five, then all went forth to view the illuminations, which presented a Monte Christo effect at night—the most charming and beautiful scene I ever witnessed, as a varied and magnificent luminance.

Miss Tessie O'Meara, who is the soul of hospitality, manifests a cheerfulness in dispensing it that is fascinatingly magnetic. She invites us to her "sweet home" for a few hours, where we pleasantly discuss our trip over a menu of unexcelled delicacy and liberal provision, after which, with a little music and *conversazione*, we discover the hours far advanced and take the cars at the door for the Southern. Mr. John O'Meara gracefully shares with his sister the happy privilege of dispensing the honors of the house, and I judge him to be a man of lofty principles, whose character, I'm told, soars above reproach. The mainstay and strength of the household, he lovingly assists in rocking the "cradle of declining age," for his gentle mother is advanced to the years of Dr. Oliver Wendell Homes, and celebrates her birthday on the same date with the venerable author.

October 4.

We attempted to attend mass at nine o'clock, but the hour has been changed for the summer. I feel very weak and feverish, and am obliged to keep my room for the day. Had my dinner upstairs, but at four o'clock am prepared for the evening, when we shall take our departure for the far West. Mrs. Murphy and the rest attended mass, then spent some time at the Convent of the Sacred Heart, at Maryville, and returned at five. After supper our St. Louis friends attend us to the Union Depot, and at 8:15 we enter the "Clebourne" sleeper, and, having crossed the river, retire for the night.

October 5.

Awoke this morning in St. Joseph's, an extensive city, but at one time a modest trading post. It was to this vicinity, I believe, that our pioneers first drifted. They then settled in Atchison County, which, being subdivided, located them in Holt County, after which they determined to go farther west, and successfully reached our peerless sunland. The remains of Grandmother Murphy rest in Missouri soil, therefore the grand old State has a claim to our reverence and affection.

Our attentive, generous, patient escort, Mr. Shriver, parts with us here, after carefully attending to the details of our baggage, and making everything as easy as possible for us. He has been most kind and thoughtful for our comfort, yet the "best of friends must part."

Steaming over the southernmost line of Nebraska, we find it dried and bleak looking, illy comparing with its fresh green appearance of two months ago. Here it is raining. A heavy, leaden sky throws a gray gloom over the landscape. We are on the Burlington and Missouri River Railroad until we reach Denver, then change to another sleeper, this one returning to St. Louis.

Tuesday, October 6.

In Nebraska we encounter snow; it is everywhere visible to Denver, where we are brought to a sudden halt by our engine jumping the track, and we stop with a quick jolt. Ordering a carriage, Mrs. Murphy takes charge, and we are rapidly deposited at the Union Depot, where she secures passage on the next train to Salt Lake. Breakfasting at the depot restaurant, the steward comes forward to inquire regarding our whereabouts since he had seen us at the Windsor two months ago. We are all amused, and Evie's countenance is submerged in laughter.

On the "Buda" vestibule car we resume our journey. Snow, snow, snow, on every side. The mountain steeps, rugged and wild, are wrapped in soft white blankets of snow, and as we approach the great Royal Gorge of the Arkansas, we take seats at the rear of the car to get the benefit of the view. The cliffs seem very familiar to me, so indelibly impressed are they upon my memory. The rest of the party seem very well, but I feel weary and weak. We lunched on the cars at Palmer Lake, and dined at Salida, Monte Christo Hotel, where we had a good warm meal.

CHAPTER XVII.

SALT LAKE CITY.

Wednesday, October 7.

WE are up at 7 o'clock and breakfast at Palmer House, near the desert. A few miles more and we cross Green River and come upon the desert, which we traveled over by night before. It is a lengthy stretch of desolate, sandy country, with only here and there tufts of desert grass. Sand is drifting everywhere, and the eye only meets desolation as it wanders in search of an oasis.

We reach Price about eleven o'clock and lunch on the car, as we pass through Castle Gate. Here a jewelry vender enters our parlors and Mrs. Murphy purchases spoons, etc. Evie asked the name of a station, and the itinerant jeweler answered, "'Helper,' and don't *you* think one needs a *helper* here?" Evie collapsed.

The foliage has all changed. The gorgeous dyes of Autumn, the full-blown matron of the year, are in strong contrast with the green of two short months ago. Only industry and

Mormonism could thrive in this sage-ridden country. The Book Mountains are a curiosity indeed, the strata, or layers, lying like books, even and continuous, and they carry the eye along in wonder until the next bowlder repeats the last or reaches more determinedly to cloudland.

At two o'clock we steam along through the happily reclaimed Great Salt Lake Valley, which is again extended before us for miles under greenswards and teeming orchards. The city of Zion gained at four o'clock, we listen to the repetition of Albany's confusion of hackmen, and finally secure the Walker House coach. At the hotel I find a letter awaiting me from Josie, which, of course, I eagerly read.

Mrs. Murphy ordered a carriage, and we were driven by a cockney coachman all over the city, and, being glib of tongue and full of wit, we had double benefit in our sight-seeing. Temple Square incloses the tabernacle and temple, but their doors had just been closed, and we were deprived of an interesting sight. The Assembly House is also a feature in this square of fine buildings. Thence we viewed all the late Brigham Young's possessions, his own grounds being defended by an adobe and stone wall. The graveyard where lie his remains is in the center of the town almost, and beside him repose six of his wives. "The rest are with the prophets." We were shown two of his daughters and a son and I think about a *thousand* sons-in-law and other connections. The Tithe house adjoins Brigham Young's dwelling, but the Endowment house has been burned down. The far-famed prophet Young had been the father of sixty-one children, but only eighteen were living at the time of his death—enough, however, to perpetuate his name.

We saw three of the twelve disciples. There is nothing suggestive of religious dignity in their bearing or manner. Mormonism has been somewhat bettered of late years. The Edmunds Bill, considerable legislation, and Mrs. Walker's and Miss Kate Field's lectures have all contributed towards the amelioration of the deluded Mormon women, who formerly were the slaves of the elders. The number of wives is limited, and the husband is required to support all properly. It is said that some of the elders' wives agree perfectly, drive out together, dine, and call, and tender to each the courtesy of refinement and respect, whereas other wives do not even glance at each other; it is a trial of temperament and character.

From Prospect Hill we watched the sun sinking down the western sky, its brilliant gleams reflected most gorgeously in the calm, broad waters of Great Salt Lake; it was a beautiful picture. The Jordan winds its way to the lake.

We are in the city of Zion; the apostles are here. May it not be the New Jerusalem? Yet no, for the *Jews are Gentiles* here. Well, it is a fine city. The streets are one hundred and thirty-five feet wide, with twenty feet for sidewalks. The trees are thrifty, varied, and numerous. We are shown the residence of Bishop Scanlan, built of brick, with stone front, also the church.

After a look at Fort Douglas, the rough spurs of the Uintahs, the pass through which the hardy Mormons entered the valley, we return to the Walker and dine. We take a room for the night, and at 12:30 P. M. we are ready for the West-bound train, whereon Mrs. Murphy has secured a drawing room. Upon presenting our tickets, however, it is discovered that the drawing room has been sold in Chicago through to California, so we hearken to an animated discussion between the guilty agent and Mrs. Murphy, and the mistake is finally adjusted after we reach Ogden. They give us three lower berths, so, at two o'clock, we claim them, very weary-eyed and languid.

CHAPTER XVIII.

HOME AGAIN.

Thursday, October 8.

AWOKE at Terrace, Nevada. The same old bleak, bald pate of the prairie looms up before us, and the wings of desolation, folded since we left the Colorado desert, have been flapped over this dreary, lonesome place. Our breakfast is served from the buffet. The porter informs us that we shall reach San Francisco at 9:15 tomorrow morning, which for me means that I gain the threshold of home in the evening, and be again amongst my loved ones. It seems so long since I left them, and in the quietude of that happy scene of serenity and love, I shall experience indescribable pleasure in relating the incidents of this tour and the enjoyment it has afforded me.

We reached Elko at noon, and received the San Francisco papers, looking at them as into the faces of familiar acquaintances. I have felt ill all day, and as night draws her mantle, am ready for repose. There are several peculiar characters on board. who present a different phase of life to those unsophisticated in its ways, as myself, and they are a source of disgust to us.

Friday, October 9.

During the night we passed over the Sierras, and I have again missed seeing them. At five o'clock this morning we stopped at Sacramento, and we rise, dress for sight-seeing, and behold the broad bosom of the Sacramento Valley bared before us. There is a familiar look to the country. and erelong we steam into Benicia, thence crossing on the *Solano*, whose motion is hardly perceptible. The serrated peninsula of Marin lies dreamily on our right, the calm blue waters of San Pablo laving its base, as they shine in the morning sunlight.

At 9:15 we step off the ferryboat at the foot of Market Street, and friends near and dear greet us home, and we keenly realize that

"'Mid pleasures and palaces," etc.,
"There's no place like home."

And now my companions go south to San Jose, and I turn north to San Rafael, each filled with happy memories of pleasure given and received.

www.ingramcontent.com/pod-product-compliance
Lightning Source LLC
Chambersburg PA
CBHW030258170426
43202CB00009B/800